Australian
Women of Grace

Australian Women of Grace tells the stories of five ordinary Australian women who have lived through a range of life experiences, from the depths of depression, cancer and sexual abuse, to the heights of being presented to the Queen, becoming a member of government and enjoying high table at Oxford.

These women represent the many who do not make headlines but who, in their daily living, by the grace of God, overcome obstacles with courage and change things for the better in their corner of the world.

*to Jane and Robyn
with God's blessings,
Ingrid*

Robyn Hipkiss

Australian Women of Grace

First published through irrePRESSible Publishing Services in 2006

Scripture quotations marked NIV are taken from *The Holy Bible, New International Version,* Copyright c 1973, 1978, 1984 by the International Bible Society. Used by permission of Zondervan Publishing House. Quotations marked KJV are taken from *The Holy Bible, King James Version.*

The National Library of Australia Cataloguing-in-Publication entry

Hipkiss, Robyn.
        Australian women of grace : stories of faith and courage.

        Bibliography.
        Includes index.
        ISBN 9780646465913.

        ISBN 0 646 46591 0.

        1. Women - Australia - Biography. 2. Spiritual biography - Australia. I. Title.

        920.720994

Orders may be obtained direct from the author:
Mrs Robyn Hipkiss, PO Box 3501, Belconnen, ACT, 2617
Email: jrhipkiss@optusnet.com.au

Cover design and layout by Caroline Ambrus
Cover photograph by Geoffrey Crook
Printed and bound by Ching Luen Printing Co. Ltd., Hong Kong

Contents

Introduction

The common theme running through all of the stories in this book presents a picture to us of an intricate tapestry being woven by a master weaver.

The rough dark threads of despair in the sad and difficult times are lightened and lifted by the golden threads of God's loving care and divine intervention. The seemingly meaningless shapes and colours of life's experiences are woven into a beautiful and complex pattern under the skilful touch of the master's hand.

Often we cannot see the design taking shape because we are too close to the fabric of our lives. But when we take the time to look back, as the women in this book have done, we can clearly see the good and bad events that have moulded our characters and made us what we are today — God's masterpiece.

Robyn Hipkiss

Acknowledgments

So often we only see the public face of people and presume they have had an easy life and everything has gone well for them. When we hear of the path they have walked, and how they overcame the challenges and difficulties in their lives, we are often amazed, inspired and encouraged.

Australian Women of Grace tells the stories of ordinary Australian women who have been an inspiration to me over the years. Although a book could be written about each one, I have provided just a glimpse into their lives, told in their own words, in the hope that their stories of faith and courage will inspire many others.

When I began writing and editing this book I had no idea it would take many hundreds of hours, over three years, to complete. This was an undertaking of greater magnitude than anything I had previously attempted. My predicament is that now the book is finally finished, I can think of many more wonderful stories I would like to tell!

I want to thank Hilary, Jenny, Betty and Ingrid, who have been willing to spend copious amounts of their time and have bared their souls to record their stories. This has involved writing out notes, taping interviews, sitting with me for many hours at the computer, and patiently answering my endless questions. By their openness they have risked the vulnerability that this brings. We have wept, laughed and prayed together as we followed their life's journey. I have endeavoured to be as accurate as possible in the recounting of events, but childhood memories are sometimes hazy, so there might be some discrepancies in dates, or gaps in the stories. Hopefully your imagination will fill in those places.

Thank you to all my friends who have been my sounding boards, proof readers and encouragers along the way. I have deeply appreciated the invaluable comments and helpful advice from Dr Barry Chant, suggestions and editorial input from Ruth Alder, Zillah Williams and Patricia Stone, and the ongoing support of Betty Hocking, a writer herself, who has constantly encouraged and patiently advised me as the book has progressed. Particular thanks to my wonderful editor, Kaaren Sutcliffe, who has pulled it all together with her fine tuning, and to Caroline Ambrus for the cover design and layout.

Most of all I want to thank God for his unfailing love and faithfulness throughout my life.

Robyn Hipkiss

Preface

In this book Robyn Hipkiss introduces us to some remarkable women – including herself – who tell how they forged their way through difficulties, setbacks, discouragements, opportunities and intimidating possibilities, and who came through on top.

Robyn is no stranger to such matters. I have known her for thirty years or more, and have witnessed her own courage and faith in difficult times. In this volume she tells, among other things, of her family's struggle with death and disease; of her battle against both her initial sense of inadequacy and the discouraging comments of others to begin a ministry that touched the lives of hundreds of children; of her gritty resolve during her husband's ill-health.

There are many untold matters as well. When I first knew Robyn, she was working as a church secretary. She was efficient, cheerful, loyal and competent. Her sincere love for God and for the church radiated from her. She was enterprising and creative and seemed to know how to stay above frustration and difficulty. My prevailing impression of her to this day is of someone possessed of a quiet joy – whenever I think of her she is always smiling.

Barry Chant

Founding President: Tabor College, Australia
Senior Pastor: Wesley International Congregation, Sydney

INGRID ROSS

I first met Ingrid at the school my children attended in the early 1980's, when she taught them German language classes with infectious enthusiasm. Through her genuine love and concern I believe she had a positive influence on the lives of many hundreds of children.

Since that time, I have come to know Ingrid personally and found her to be a vibrant woman, abounding in energy and vitality, despite her battle with severe health problems.

Ingrid exudes a warm outgoing love. Without prejudice or bias, she genuinely delights in helping all who come within her sphere. There is always room for one more at Ingrid's meal table.

Tempered by her experiences of growing up in war torn Germany, Ingrid has embraced her adopted country of Australia with great affection. This is very evident in her role as a tour guide of historic sites in Canberra.

Peace Child

INGRID'S STORY

Sirens were wailing, bombers droned in the sky, people were running for their lives – then came the dreadful silence before the bombs hit. My mother, who always had me fully dressed in coat, shoes, socks and hat, even in bed, snatched me up into her arms and ran for the nearest underground bunker, which held up to 2,000 people. We huddled together trying to comfort one another as the planes droned overhead and we listened for the siren that would give us the all clear. One dreadful night I remember a woman running with five children, trying to get into the bunker in time. But many others were running too, and one of her children was trampled to death. I still hear the mother's anguished screams.

Another night we were in the bunker for what seemed an interminably long time. Finally the all clear sounded, but our relief didn't last long. When we emerged into the night we were devastated to find that our house had been bombed. Just three years of age at the time, I remember clinging fiercely to my mother's hand while we approached what remained of our house. My mother stood in the dark, tears rolling down her cheeks and her grip on my hand vice-like. Our home, once filled with love and laughter, all our worldly possessions, mementos of our life, were gone, destroyed in a moment by the bomb and by fire. The looters were already fossicking through the blackened and charred goods as if they owned them.

CHILDHOOD MEMORIES

I was born Ingrid Beate Hartmann in Koblenz on the Rhine, in Germany, in May 1939. My parents called me the peace child, because I was born in one of the last few months of peace before World War II started. My mother's father (my Opa), who was to play a major role in my early life, lived with my grandmother (my Oma) opposite the hospital. The labour ward faced their bedroom and he was convinced he heard me scream as soon as I was born. I am sure I made a noise just to assure everyone that I was alive and well because my mother had been rammed into a window by a car shortly before my birth. I see God's mighty hand of protection in that incident. It was the first time He saved me from death.

The early years of my life were very happy. My mother, aunt and grandparents surrounded me with love and care. My father was not at home because he had been conscripted into the German army. He served as an officer, first on the western, and later on the eastern front. He only came home on leave once, for a short time when I was quite young. I walked past him on the pavement going up to the shops on an errand. He bent down to greet me (my mother had sent him pictures of me), and because I had no idea who he was I told him that I did not speak to strange men. When I returned from my shopping, he was in our kitchen holding my mother's hand. Confused by this I asked my mother, "Who is this man?" She gently explained that he was my father, home from the war for a short visit.

Although home for just a brief time, my father went out of his way to teach me many things and to show me his care and love. He took me for walks and spoke to me as an adult in a very loving way that was never condescending. As I got to know my father, I learnt to love and respect him and to appreciate his integrity of character. I have never forgotten the things my Dad imparted to me in that short period of my young life before he returned to the war zone.

Our lives were changed for ever on that fateful night in 1942 when our home and possessions were destroyed. Because of the continual bombing in Koblenz it was unsafe for us to stay there, so we sought refuge in Woelferlingen, a village in the mountains behind Koblenz, hoping to find help from uncles and aunts from my grandmother's clan. We only had the clothes on our back and a huge pram, which my mother had filled with a few basic necessities. As far as I can remember, we walked most of the thirty five kilometres to the village. We approached two households who were relatives of our family, but they would not take us in or help us in any way, and instead sent us to some people in the village who, they said, would rent us a room.

My mother and I were left to fend for ourselves, with no food and little income, in a village where the people spoke a different dialect. I don't clearly remember all the details, being so small at the time, but presume that my mother must have received a small pension from my father, and that with this she was able to rent the tiny, unheated room three metres square. This contained a bed, a cupboard, a table and chair, and a stove, which we kept burning with wood collected in the nearby forest.

My mother was not daunted by this. She tackled the problems with imagination and improvisation. To my child's eye, it seemed that she pulled tricks out of her hat like a magician. She taught me how to dig for potatoes without getting a sore back; how to pick up stinging nettles with gloves so as not to get stung and itch for hours (these were our spinach intake); how to cut off the green growth on a small pine tree and cook it for honey; how to ask the farmers for a few beets so that we could juice them and get thickened treacle; how to glean in the fields like Ruth did in the Bible story, and take the ears of wheat to a miller who was kind enough to mill them into flour for us; how to dig for dandelion roots so that, after soaking them for a day, we could eat them like a chicory salad. Yum! We made a lot of soup, and to this day I still like soup. We had a big pot on the stove, which made cooking easy. My mother was the most astonishing, active, enthusiastic and happy person that you could imagine. She never uttered a negative word or showed any grief over the loss of our possessions, and never once moaned over the less than congenial living conditions.

My mother was a superb dressmaker. She started to make dresses for a few important people in the village, which they showed off at the village dance. Mum became the most popular person in the village. She began to bargain, and would only go to peoples' homes to sew if in return we were given milk, butter, meat and some blood sausages when they slaughtered cattle. When mum was sewing at the farmer's house we were allowed to eat with the family each day because she was able to sew for the men as well as the women. God was faithful and supplied all our needs.

There was much to be grateful for, but my deformed toes are a lasting reminder of those days. For two years I had to force my feet into wooden clogs or ill-fitting second-hand shoes in an effort to combat the minus 20°c winter temperatures on the heights above Koblenz. Instead of growing normally, my toes became deformed. This makes buying shoes something of a nightmare.

My grandparents' home was bombed in 1945 and they were also evacuated to Woelferlingen. Although a terrible experience for them, it proved to be a blessing for me. Now I had a father figure in my life. My Opa was the most wonderfully patient man you could wish for, always ready to listen, and he could repair anything that was damaged, even emotions!

After I had learned the dialect, I gathered up the children from the village, some of whom were also evacuees, and formed a dramatic society. I was about eight years old at the time. We didn't have school every day so we had plenty of time to amuse ourselves. I loved organising events, and had lots of energy and a love of the dramatic. We produced an original play every fortnight, based on life in the village, for which we charged entrance fees. This brought a bit of cash into the family. If people couldn't pay they brought vegetables or bread.

FATHER RETURNS

When I was nine years old, in 1948, to my great joy, my father returned home. My mother had heard about arrangements being made by the Red Cross to transport soldiers home from the prisoner of war camps, and she obtained a permit to fetch my father. Germany had been divided into zones by this time. We were in the French zone. Because travelling was so difficult, Mum dyed her hair and made herself look old, instead of a beautiful 37-year-old, and hitched a ride with our mayor, who was allowed to travel from zone to zone. Three weeks later she was reunited with my father. When my father realised what a dangerous situation she had placed herself in he was not pleased, but this was eclipsed by their great happiness at being together again.

Father had been captured in 1945, with 25,000 men under his command, and was sent to a labour camp in Minsk, then in the Soviet Union, and now the capital of Belorus. He had suffered greatly because he was made to work in freezing conditions of minus 30°c at the labour camp. Fortunately, an old-fashioned Russian officer took a liking to my Dad. This officer had been in German captivity in World War I and had been fitted by a German doctor with a prosthesis for his missing leg. The prosthesis was so good that his slight limp was hardly visible. His attitude towards the prisoners was tempered by this experience. He organised penicillin for my father when he contracted diphtheria, without which he would have died. I thank

God for this man who had a kind and compassionate heart. On my father's return from the war he spoke well of this man, and also of the many women who came to the perimeter of the camp and pushed a cooked potato or an onion under the fence. In later years my father still loved onions, even though they made him sick, because to him they were a sign of love reaching across the borders of different nationalities. He felt that he had seen the true spirit and the caring heart of the Russian people.

My father was a physically broken man with a body weight of just thirty three kilos, even though he was taller than my 1.70m. His arms were tightly swollen with fluid because of the constant diet of watery soup. The Soviets finally agreed to send him back because he had become useless as a worker.

Mum took him to stay with relatives for two months while they slowly fed him and helped him begin to recuperate from nine years of war and labour camp. We were so thankful that he had come back to us. So many other dads, uncles and sons never returned to their families. He spent the rest of his life trying to forget the horrors of the war. Despite all he had been through, my father did not become cynical or bitter, but retained his wisdom and integrity, along with a keen discernment of human nature.

SCHOOL DAYS

In 1949, when I was ten years old, I had to take the entrance exam for the Montabaur Gymnasium (grammar school) and because my birth certificate had been burnt on that fateful night of the bombing I almost missed out on taking the exam. Fortunately, we were able to locate the doctor who could certify the date of my birth. As I had only attended primary school twice a week my mother had supplemented my education by teaching me at home as much as she was able. However, she had forgotten to teach me fractions, and they were a big part of the maths paper. During the exam, since I had never seen fractions before in my life, I was curious and looked at my neighbour's paper. Oops, this was a bad move! My paper was snatched from me by the invigilator and I was sent out of the room. My father bought me my first ever ice-cream to console me. To everyone's great relief, I was admitted to the grammar school in Montabaur despite the mishap.

When the school term began, I got up at five each morning, walked nine kilometres to the railway station and caught two trains to start school at eight a.m. When school finished at one thirty p.m. I did the whole journey in reverse and finally got home at five p.m. Thankfully there were three other children from the village who also had to complete this daily marathon. However, six months later I was so exhausted and had lost so much weight that my mother realised she would have to find another solution for my schooling or I would not survive. She made enquiries, and eventually found me accommodation with Frau Hillersheim in the city of Montabaur, near the school.

Frau Hillersheim lived in a very isolated house with shutters on all the windows that rattled and made strange noises during the night. The family went out two or three nights a week to various musical events and left me at home by myself. As the shutters rattled and the wind howled, my imagination conjured up images terrifying to a small girl alone in the house. I was so frightened I cried myself to sleep night after night. Travelling home on the weekends was a great blessing, but every Monday morning, when I faced the return trip I clung to my mother, pleading that I did not want to go back to school.

"Hush, hush" my mother would say. "You must have an education."

"But I'd rather be with you!" I'd wail.

"You must be brave, little Ingrid. We will be together soon."

And so my mother would persuade me, and I'd tilt my chin and get on the train.

When my father was well enough to return to work in 1949, he took up his old job as a legal public servant at the Palace of Justice, looking after civil law cases in the city of Koblenz. At first he lived in a very small room. As soon as he was able to rent a larger room I went to live with him. I left the grammar school in Montabaur and transferred to one in Koblenz called Hilda-Schule. I remember that my father had my plaits cut off because he could not manage them, and had my hair permed, which was a frizzy disaster. A few months later he was able to rent a larger three bedroom flat, then my mother joined us and we were able to live together as a family. This brought great happiness to all of us. My parents continued to live in that flat until their old age. I learnt to play the piano, bought by father with great personal sacrifice, and found release and expression through playing it. Many years later, when I moved to Australia as an adult, my father had the piano shipped over to me so that I could have my own piano in my own home. This was such a loving gesture and brought with it many happy memories.

My father was a wonderful example to me in so many ways. One instance in particular stands out in my memory. We had travelled on the train together, and my father was so impressed with the clarity of a young woman's announcement over the public address system (instead of the usual garbled words that no-one understood), that he took the time to write a letter to officials at the railway station asking them to highly commend her. He received a reply saying they had found the girl and passed on his positive comments, and that she was very grateful. This small incident was just one of many examples my father showed me about the importance of taking the time to encourage and commend those who come across our path. Throughout my life I have always endeavoured to follow my father's example by expressing my appreciation of services given.

I lived with my parents and attended school until I matriculated. There was no bus service so I walked approximately four kilometres to school every day, carrying a bag filled with heavy school books. As we lived on the other side of the River Rhine from the school, I walked about a kilometre to the top of the hill, and then down a staircase with 495 steps. I always jumped down the steps in twos all the way to the bottom, accomplishing this in a matter of minutes, and then walked across the bridge over the wide river to finish the rest of the journey to school. I am sure that the constant jarring of jumping down those 495 steps every day for many years damaged my knees, which is probably why I have such problems with them now. Coming home from school I would struggle back up the stairs again, in heat, cold, ice and snow. It certainly toughened me up.

TEENAGE YEARS.

My grandfather died when I was thirteen and I was heartbroken. It was just two weeks before my Lutheran confirmation and I can remember hollering within myself at God and asking the famous "why" question. However, at the confirmation service I said "Ja" to God, along with all the other children and, looking back now, I know that this was the beginning of my walk with Him. I felt very keenly that I had to give my heart to God.

I enjoyed a full, active and happy life during my teenage years. I played tennis and competed at the rowing club for four years. Bike riding was another favourite pastime, and my friends and I completed very long bike rides, some of up to 700 kilometres, riding 100 kilometres in one day if the road was fairly flat. Having a love of drama and the theatre, I found great fulfilment in being part of the school dramatic society and productions. In one play I had to fight a fencing duel, so I went to fencing lessons and loved them so much I decided to keep learning. My mother continued her role as a home-maker, as well as sewing all our clothes for us. My father was superbly dressed, probably the best dressed man in the neighbourhood. Sometimes in the mornings I would find hanging in the wardrobe a new dress that Mum had run up for me overnight.

Some special events were the beautiful balls organised by the rowing club, which the boys and girls from the grammar schools and their parents attended. This was a wonderful opportunity for us to dress up in our long gowns, and to dance and socialise with other young people as well as with their parents. We also had private house balls. We held a number in our flat, when all the rooms were cleared out and we utilised the large communal outside area between the flats. One ball I remember in particular was a carnival ball when everyone came in costume. It was absolutely beautiful. My mother had cooked for days on end. She made the most fantastic gateaux, and the parents enjoyed the evening as much as we did. We often danced until two in the morning.

In the last two years of my nine years at grammar school I was preparing for the Higher School

Certificate examinations (known in Germany as the Abitur). At that time it guaranteed automatic entrance to University. I and my friends had an incredibly heavy study load with five core subjects plus another nine minor subjects. When it came to the final exam time and my marks from the last two years were added up, it was found that they were not sufficient and that I was not going to be admitted to the Abitur. I had no idea why my marks did not add up highly enough, and I was terribly shocked. I had worked extremely hard at my studies and had done well enough throughout the two years. I thought I had met the required standard. There were other girls who were of a similar standard to me, but they were admitted and passed their exam. A number of reasons for this were suggested to me in later years. However, at the time I had no explanation and was devastated and bewildered.

My parents realised the terrible effect this had on me because I was the only one in my class to be excluded. In those days the German Grammar school programme was inflexible and authoritarian, and my parents were intimidated by the system and did not feel they could appeal this decision. They took me out of school immediately and sent me to my aunt's home in the mountains. For the next three months I tutored her three sons in almost every subject. This restored my confidence, which had all but been destroyed, as well as improving my subject knowledge.

Because it was the only Protestant Grammar

school in our area, with a high academic standard, I returned to the school after the holiday break. This was a difficult time for me, but I was fortunate to make a very good friend in the first few days. She stood by me while I adjusted and overcame the stigma of joining a younger class.

Through this experience I learnt some valuable lessons about life. I gained a new understanding of mathematics from a gifted teacher, and whereas in the past this had been one of my weaker subjects, I now achieved excellent results and went on to further studies of mathematics at university. Through my pain I also came to appreciate the suffering that can be experienced by students at the hands of teachers, and a desire was born in my heart to be a teacher who would love and care for her students through thick and thin, during both the good times and the bad.

MEETING MALCOLM

At nineteen years of age I matriculated and went to Freiburg University, where I started training to become a high school teacher. Eighteen months later I continued my studies at Munich University. I joined the *Kurrende,* a student choir associated with the Protestant church. The students in the choir often got together for weekend outings, especially skiing. Five of us, three girls and two boys, planned to go skiing one weekend. The hut was booked, the transport arranged and the skis waxed and ready. However, I reluctantly had to forgo the trip because an important oral exam was looming on the

Monday. It would determine whether my scholarship was extended or cancelled, and as I wasn't certain that I had revised enough, I stayed behind to study. Tragically, during one of the day's skiing the girls took a different route from the boys and were buried alive by an avalanche. The rescuers were not able to get them out in time. This was the second time God saved me from certain death.

I wanted to get away from Munich and improve my English, so I applied to study for two terms at Bristol University in the United Kingdom. One Saturday night in late September 1962, I arrived at the residence. It was an Anglo-Catholic home run by nuns. There were nine other girls in residence, so I would be able to practise my English. I shared a room with an English girl named Elizabeth, who was very 'top-drawer'.

One day, she said to me in her most proper English accent, "Ingrid, do you realise that you speak with very guttural sounds – and that you speak in German while you are asleep?"

To which I replied, "Nein, Elizabeth, I hadn't realised."

Six weeks later, she said, "I say, Ingrid, do you know that you spoke in English in your sleep last night – how very jolly!"

I knew then that I had started to break through the language barrier.

I began to get to know the other students in the residence and became friendly with Jenny, who was in a wheelchair because she had become paralysed after a riding accident. She had been a sportswoman and, realising that I was fit and ready for adventure, she suggested that I might like to join the students from the University Explorers' Club, who went bushwalking every Sunday. She was so keen for me to become involved that I decided I would go the next Sunday. There were about 30 students in the club, and we hiked through the beautiful undulating Somerset countryside, stopping for lunch in a country pub afterwards.

During lunch I met Malcolm, a fellow university student who was on the walk. He was a sad-looking young man, dressed in an interesting selection of non-matching clothes, and I was immediately drawn to him. I thought, "I want to get to know him. He looks like he needs me to cheer him up." We ate some food together, walked and talked all afternoon, then rode home on a double-decker bus. On the way home Malcolm asked me out for a coffee that night, but in my strong German accent I said, "Nein! Zat vill not do as I am going to the Cassedral for ze beginning of ze term service – aren't you coming?"

He agreed to come, even though he hadn't been inside a church for three years. He had been brought up in a God-fearing household, but for him faith was not real. He asked how he would know me amongst the crowd and I told him I would wear my very large beefeater hat. He spotted me straight away. Indeed, it would have been impossible to miss me. After the service we had our cup of coffee, and he insisted on taking me home on the bus. He missed the last bus home and had to walk the ten kilometres to his digs. That happened on more than one occasion!

Malcolm and I spent every free waking moment getting to know one another, studying in the library, eating in the refectory, attending lectures, and working together. We had some interesting and hilarious moments as our relationship developed, with my use of certain German words which had very different meanings in English. I remember Malcolm being shocked a few days after we met when I asked him if I could remove my girdle as it was too tight and uncomfortable. He was greatly relieved to discover that I only removed my belt, as the German word for belt is *guertel*! Malcolm, who was completing a major in English language and literature, helped me to overcome my guttural German accent and I soon began to think in English, a sure sign that I was mastering the language. We got to know one another well in the next five months, and in the process Malcolm started to come to a faith in God that was real and meaningful.

Malcolm's parents and his twin brothers accepted me warmly and welcomed me into their home. They were a reserved and quiet English family, and I think they were impressed by this bubbly, outgoing German girl who was dating their son. Malcolm's family lived in a semi-detached four bedroom home with a lovely big garden, beautiful flower beds and a large vegetable patch. Malcolm's mother was an excellent cook, and quite prepared to venture into exotic recipes. Malcolm's father, although quiet, had a good sense of humour and winked at me several times at the dinner table, which made me relax and feel accepted. Malcolm's twin brothers, thirteen at the time, were only used to communicating with each other, so our conversations were restricted to, "Dunno," "Maybe" and "Yep". This has now changed and we communicate really well.

Eartha Kitt used to sing that "an Englishman needs time", but Malcolm proposed to me six weeks after that Sunday bushwalk. Although he was studious and extremely shy, he was very much in love. He had been concerned about a ring I was wearing, that my parents had given me after a very good examination result, and asked me if I was engaged. When I answered in the negative, I believe it spurred him on to pursue me. We were returning from a trip to London, when we had to change buses. Malcolm proposed while we were sitting on a public bench waiting for the next bus to arrive. I am not sure why he chose that moment and place, but I had no hesitation in accepting his proposal with much delight.

In the April of 1963 I returned to Germany to start my summer term, and Malcolm came with me because he wanted to meet my parents and to ask my father formally for my hand in marriage. This was going to be difficult since Malcolm's German was still poor and my father's English was limited. I spoke to my father and said he should not make it difficult for Malcolm, and suggested that he just ask questions to which Malcolm could answer "yes" or "no". I then devised a clever scheme to help Malcolm answer the questions correctly. I seated myself in the bathroom, which was located right next to the lounge room, and had conveniently thin walls. Malcolm sat near the bathroom wall. For each of the questions I would tap once for no and twice for yes. Malcolm completed the interview successfully and our future was assured! He then flew back to England to continue his studies, and I returned to study in Munich. This need to communicate with my family spurred Malcolm on to master the German language, and all my friends were impressed that he could speak German with hardly a mistake.

We were engaged for more than two years, during which time we continued with our studies and wrote a letter to each other every day. We were married in 1965 in Koblenz. My mother made my elegant wedding gown which was a very simple A-line dress with a lace jacket. The veil had not been tried on beforehand, and was somehow fixed quickly on my head a few minutes before leaving for the church. Unfortunately I had no hairdresser or photographer, because they both forgot to come. Although the wedding party was not very large we were happy that all our family, both from the UK and Germany, were there to celebrate this special occasion with us. While we were saying our wedding vows in the church I began to feel unwell, and whispered to Malcolm, "Hold me tight, I am going to faint." Throughout the rest of the service Malcolm held me firmly in his arms, which

27

everyone thought was so romantic. We were just hoping I would stay conscious for the remainder of the celebration. The reception was held in a lovely restaurant overlooking the Rhine. After staying on for two days after the wedding to help our in-laws communicate with one another, because of the language difficulties, we spent our honeymoon in Prague, and had a precious time being together at last.

Malcolm obtained a teaching position at the Munich city language school, which was an excellent placement. I taught in Garmisch-Partenkirchen in the German Alps. We had an unusual beginning to our marriage. Malcolm travelled up on the train on a Thursday night, we had the long weekend together, then he returned to Munich on the Monday afternoon. This was made possible with the help of the Director of the language school who arranged a compressed teaching timetable for Malcolm, for which we were very grateful.

TEACHING EXPERIENCES

We worked and lived like this for seven months, then decided to return to Bristol. I applied for a scholarship there to complete my teacher's certificate, which involved a year of study and a term of teaching, and was accepted. My teaching practice took place at a comprehensive school in a poor socio-economic area of Bristol. This was a new school system, through which children who had failed the required examination for entrance into a selective high school could be educated right up to university entrance level.

I was given a fourth-form class for geography with a curriculum that included teaching about the wheat belt of America. I soon discovered that it was the most difficult class in the school. They played cards, sat with their feet up on the tables, and were not interested in taking any notice of the teacher at the front of the class. I was twenty five at the time and had some teaching experience in Germany. I went to the Headmaster with a plan. I suggested to him that it seemed to be a pointless exercise trying to teach these fourteen-year-olds information and knowledge that they felt was totally irrelevant and of little value to them. We made a pact that, once I got their attention, I would teach them life skills to increase their self confidence and provide them with practical knowledge that would benefit them in their future lives.

For the next ten days I took a novel to school with me, which I pretended to read during the geography classes, while ignoring the students. This aroused their curiosity until eventually one of them said, "Hey, Miss, are you ever gonna teach us somethin?"

To which I responded, "Do you want to learn?"

When the answer to this question was positive, I had a long and fruitful discussion with the class. We worked out a syllabus together that included cooking, etiquette, sex education, how to fill in forms, interview techniques, and much more. At the end of the term

Malcolm and I invited the students to dinner at our home and we were delighted to see how they presented themselves and behaved during the evening. They had become much more confident young men and women who were now better prepared for the challenges life would throw at them.

****

During my education year I was invited to do a Master of Arts but, as Malcolm had already started on his Master of Letters, I deferred my degree, forever, as it turned out. At this time I was invited to teach at an open prison, a prison without walls, where the inmates were encouraged to take outside courses to prepare them for their release. I had a class of five inmates and I was to teach them German to year ten standard (O Level). They had been imprisoned for various crimes such as stealing, cracking and hiding a safe, embezzlement, robbery with violence, and receiving stolen cars. During my weekly trips to the prison I got to know each of them very well as I learnt their stories. I taught them a very intense one-year course of German, which they all passed.

At the end of the year Malcolm and I sought Home Office approval to invite the prisoners for dinner at our home, where we planned to introduce them to our friends in Bristol. Approval was granted. It became a complicated exercise because we did not want any neighbours, or our friends, to know that they were prisoners. The evening was highly successful. My friends from the prison had somehow obtained new clothes and were very smartly dressed, and because of the knowledge they had gleaned from the prison library, were able to hold their own in conversations during the evening – even though some of their pronunciations had interesting overtones! After they left, one at a time, to meet the prison van waiting at the top of the road, our University colleagues were amazed to discover where I had met this new group of friends. They never thought about prisoners in quite the same way again.

A surprise visit by one of the prisoners is one of the most precious Christmas gifts I have ever received. He came back to see us three years after his release from prison, on Christmas Eve, to introduce us to his wife. He told us that he had started a business making concrete walls, called Fincon. The name could be interpreted either as 'finished concrete' or 'finished convict'. His wife knew about his past and fully supported him.

A FAMILY AT LAST

Malcolm and I had been trying for some time to have a child, but without success. The doctors did all the tests and could find no medical reason for this. The feelings I experienced during this time were as if I was rushing down to catch a cruise ship at the quay that would take me on an exciting adventure, only to discover when I finally reached the harbour that the ship was out of reach and had left without me. I could see the streamers drifting down onto the water, people waving goodbye to their loved ones, and I stood among them lost, sad and bitterly disappointed. One week I thought I was pregnant and I began to imagine what it would be like to carry my own child, only to have my hopes dashed. This caused us great pain and heartache.

Finally, in 1968, over the Christmas holiday period, we decided to apply for adoption. Nine months later a nondescript envelope arrived among many others and I put it right at the bottom of the pile. Imagine my surprise when I finally opened it and discovered that it contained the wonderful news that a little baby girl was waiting for us in London! I was so excited I couldn't wait to share the news with Malcolm so I rang him at the school, but he was teaching a class. I then rang my mother in Germany, but her phone line was engaged. I tried my mother-in-law in London, but she was out. I finally got into the car, drove to the school, and rushed into the staff room, where I discovered Malcolm standing with a group of his colleagues. I announced at the top of my voice, "Darling, we are pregnant!" He was slightly embarrassed, but delighted with the news.

Three days later, after much excited preparation, we drove to London – nervous and expectant. Malcolm picked up Pippa and she immediately seized his glasses and stroked him tenderly. He fell for her on the spot. She was a beautiful baby and we showed her off proudly to everyone. God had given us a child!

Two years later we took the same journey, accompanied by our two-year-old daughter. Pippa was the first to be introduced to gorgeous baby James and to proudly call him, "My baby brother". Now we were a complete family, and so grateful to our Father in Heaven that He had blessed us with two beautiful children.

We shared some precious family times with my parents when they came from Germany to visit us. On one visit we went for a holiday to South Wales and stayed in a spacious caravan overlooking the sea. Once the children were in bed we would sit and talk, and one night we tumbled onto the subject of eternity. With tears in my eyes, I endeavoured to make clear to my Dad that my heart's desire was to see him acknowledge God and find a personal relationship with Him. I said to him, "Dad, because I love you so much I want to know that you will be with me in heaven when the time comes for us to leave this earth." That was the first time I ever saw my father cry.

PAPUA NEW GUINEA

In January 1973 we were on a plane undertaking a 48-hour journey to Rabaul in Papua New Guinea, where Malcolm had taken a position as Head of English at Kerevat Senior High School, thirty kilometres from Rabaul. We lived in a two-bedroom house on stilts right opposite the girls' dorm. It was noisy, but great fun. The stilts were important as there could be up to ten earthquakes a week, when the house would swing and the fridge would walk! We did not have a rainwater tank, so we had to boil every drop of water before we could use it. There were no fans, which was disastrous when it was extremely hot and humid. The bedroom walls faced west and in the afternoon they were so hot you couldn't touch them.

When we arrived we were not only given our house, but also a house boy, who had been contracted by a neighbour to work for us. Kieta, who came from the Highlands, only spoke his own language and Pidgin. I had a limited understanding of Pidgin at that time, and this produced some interesting communication problems.

One morning he asked me a question, which sounded to my ears like, "Missis, me like kissim leg bilong you?"

Since I assumed that he wanted to kiss my leg I screamed and ran out of the house, straight to Malcolm's classroom. When I retold the story the whole class dissolved into hysterical laughter. As it turned out, he was actually saying, "Mi laik kissim lek bilong yu?" which actually meant, "Can I borrow your grass rake?" This became a standing joke amongst our friends. My grasp of Pidgin improved rapidly after this.

Soon the word spread that we were Lutherans and a group of fifteen students began to meet in our house for fellowship and Bible study. At the first meeting I offered them coffee and cake, and as I was passing the milk around I asked casually, "Are you black or white?" Thank goodness they appreciated the unintended pun and burst out laughing, breaking the ice! Two of them asked us independently whether we would be their Mum and Dad. We were surprised at this, and asked friends who had lived there for some years what it meant. They explained that this was a Melanesian way of acquiring an additional set of parents to whom they could belong and be mentored, taught and loved by. So we became Mama and Papa to these two, and in varying degrees, to another 100 students over the next ten years. We took the two with us to Europe for nine weeks and introduced them to our parents, friends and neighbours as well as to skiing and special events in Munich. One of these students, Mait, invited us back to his village the same year. Then we really became family.

Malcolm and I regularly visited Mait's home on Karkar Island to spend time with the family who had adopted us into their clan. Malcolm chose Karkar Island as the site for his linguistic research, and we have since been there many times. At one stage we counselled and prayed with Mait and his wife Irion for their shaky marriage, which is now very harmonious. We prayed with their four children, Malcolm, Nigel, Ingrid, and Louise, when they were smaller. Over the years Mait improved his house and property tremendously, and when we went to visit we were treated like royalty. We had our own bedroom with a king-sized bed constructed by a local carpenter, and a mosquito net. The toilet, a pit latrine, was fifty metres from the house, and at night this meant climbing over pigs, huge green frogs and other animals. We quickly looked for other solutions. There was no running water, so we flew in a water tank. Mait and Irion's children were very bright and Mait wanted them to have a good education. We were able to help them with school fees.

We stayed at Keravat Senior High School for two years, and at the end of that time I had lost so much weight that I fitted into size eight clothes. Malcolm was concerned about my health and sent me to see a doctor for a check-up.

When I saw the doctor he said, "Mrs Ross, I am very concerned about your health and would like to do some tests to see what the problem is."

I agreed to this, and when I was called back in to the doctor's surgery, he sat me down and said, "Mrs Ross, the test results indicate that there is a growth on your ovary, which needs to be removed as soon as possible. I think it may be cancerous and recommend immediate surgery."

He gave us that information on a Friday, and I then had a long weekend to dwell on this piece of news and its possible ramifications. I decided to go ahead with the surgery at the Catholic Mission Hospital in Kokopo, which was run by German nuns and an eccentric Irish surgeon, who phoned Malcolm after the operation and told him that he had "whipped it all out". This was a great shock as we had not been prepared for radical surgery.

I made a good recovery, and two weeks later we were on the plane with our children travelling to Europe to visit both sets of parents, taking with us our two Papua New Guinean children, Mait and Erica. Due to an oversight by the nurse not all of my stitches had been removed, and the remaining suture had allowed an infection in my wound, causing pus to drain continually from the opening during the trip. This was extremely uncomfortable and painful. Fortunately, on our arrival we were able to seek immediate medical attention. A consultant was able to quickly locate the offending suture and remove it, allowing the wound to close and heal within a short time.

After two years at Keravat we moved to Goroka in the Highlands, with a temperate and beautiful climate 1800 metres above sea level. For me it was like living in eternal spring with lovely cooler evening temperatures. Malcolm eventually became principal of the Teachers' College there. This came about in a miraculous way. When the Principal resigned and the new person selected could not take up the appointment, friends hassled Malcolm to apply for the position, even though it was a much higher level than his current one. However, we felt that we needed a definite sign from God (like Gideon's fleece in the Bible) to show us that this was His direction for our lives, as by that time Malcolm had already applied for a lecturing position at the University of Singapore.

We asked God to give us two confirmations to show us that Malcolm should consider the position of Principal. These were that, without applying for the job, Malcolm would receive a telephone call, and also a letter, offering him the position. Requests which, at the time, seemed absolutely impossible. After this, we rang the University of Singapore to enquire whether an offer had been made to Malcolm for that position. We were assured that it had, and that a letter had been sent to us in the mail, although we had not yet received it. Shortly afterwards the Vice-Chancellor of the University of PNG rang to offer Malcolm the position of Principal, and sent the letter of offer by courier. We received that offer the next day.

We felt that this was a clear direction from God and Malcolm accepted the position. The next day the letter from the University of Singapore arrived. It had taken six weeks to reach us, which was most unusual. Malcolm experienced many trials and difficulties during his time as Principal, but we drew courage and strength from God because we knew that He had placed us in that situation.

In 1977, while we were on study leave in the UK, God spoke to both of us independently about baptism by full immersion. After our baptismal service a friend gave us some words of encouragement that he felt were from God. He said, "You will bring many jewels to God's crown when you return to PNG". We put these words to the back of our minds because we couldn't see the relevance of them at that time. However, after Malcolm became College Principal, we hosted the Tertiary Students' Christian Fellowship in our home on Friday and Sunday nights and loved the ministry with the students. Usually thirty to forty students would come to worship, preach, and pray and many were saved, delivered, and healed. It was an extraordinary time, and we are still in contact with some of them. A number are now in positions of power in PNG.

By the time we left the country almost every high school had a Scripture Union group under the charge of a teacher who had been trained at the College, many of whom had spent hours in our living room. God had brought those prophetic words spoken to us at our baptism to fruition in a way we could never have imagined.

We travelled around the country quite a bit in our little four-wheel drive Subaru. One weekend we drove to Mendi in the Southern Highlands. Our children stayed with friends in Goroka. We took some Christian students as far as Mount Hagen and dropped them off for a conference. As we travelled on, the weather closed in and it poured with rain. The road from Mount Hagen to Mendi quickly deteriorated, and soon we were straddling two ruts that made up the road. Suddenly the car went into a spin and slid towards the edge of the road and a thirty metre drop. In my panic I cried out, "Jesus, save us!" The car miraculously turned the other way and ditched into the soft edge, leaving the front grill looking as if it had a crooked smile. We managed to get the Subaru out of the mud and limped into Mendi realising that God had saved us from certain death, in my case for the third time.

During our ten-year stay in PNG we travelled back to Europe every two years to see our parents and grandparents. My father so enjoyed these visits from his grandchildren, and would hide all the valuable objects and put on old trousers so that if juice was spilt on them it would not matter. My mother remained a great cook and gave us all a reprieve from my gastronomic endeavours. I feel sad now as I look back and remember how, as their only child, I lived so far away from my parents. We had literally moved to the other side of the world. However, they encouraged me to embrace life to the full, and said to me, "We want to give you wings to fly with, and roots to come back to."

In 1980 I made the visit alone, as news had reached us that Mum was very ill with an infection that had affected her whole immune system. I flew to Germany at once, but I took the flu with me. My mother, seeing how ill I was with a temperature of 41 degrees, rallied, called the doctor, and looked after me! She bathed me to bring the fever down, and fed me her sustaining home-made soups, until I was well again. Somehow, in the process, she also recovered. Once again, I shared my faith with Dad and told him about Jesus' love for him and reminded him that God had protected him during the war and brought him safely back to us. There were tears in his eyes and, after some explanation of its significance, we celebrated communion together. Mum and I had always gone to church together and later, after my father's death, she came to Australia for three months. At a church camp during that time she made a commitment to Jesus, which was the seal on a life dedicated to Him and to others.

CANBERRA

In 1982 Malcolm and I decided to leave Goroka because Pippa had reached high school age. We moved to Canberra, where Malcolm had registered to study for a Ph.D. in Linguistics at the Australian National University. He wanted a career change at the age of forty. That was quite frightening, as I had no job and Malcolm, at his age, had no scholarship.

We wanted our children to attend a Christian school and so we applied to O'Connor Christian School, which was the only one we knew that took high-school students. I took Pippa and James for an interview with the Principal, and among many other things I asked if they were introducing languages into the curriculum.

"No," he said, "We aren't."

I was shocked and asked, "How can you run a high school without a foreign language in the curriculum? That is unheard of!"

"Why are you so interested in a foreign language for your children?" he asked.

"Because I am a language teacher. I teach German, and I would like my children to learn the language," I replied.

He immediately invited me to come for an interview the following day, which was a Saturday. On

Sunday morning we attended a service at the church with which the school was associated and the Chairman of the Board told me that I had the job. So God provided a school, a job and a church in one stroke.

The school initially couldn't offer me a full-time position teaching German, so I agreed to teach something else and suggested Maths, Music, English or Social Science. They gave me Home Science for a whole year! I was horrified. I couldn't sew at all. Well, that was a challenge. Despite this, I stayed at the School for eleven years and loved it. We built up a group of students who enjoyed studying German, and for a number of years we sent students to Germany on a six-week exchange. Later, some married German-speaking boys and girls, some went evangelising in Germany and others just appreciated the experience of the exchange. It was such fun! We also ran German nights, which involved every child in the school, with the older classes writing and presenting plays in German, and the others presenting items in German in both song and dance. These bi-annual events were a great success and gave the parents an insight into language learning.

During my time at O'Connor Christian School I always encouraged the students to pray for their future spouses. This was received with much laughter and embarrassed giggles at the time. However, it has been a great joy to me many years later to be told by some of these same students that they did pray, and that God answered their prayers – as they introduced me to their future husband or wife. Even though they might not have remembered a lot of the German language, I am thankful that the seeds of faith sown into their lives have borne fruit in other ways.

A day in the life of a teacher can present many challenges. There is the need to impart knowledge, but there is also the need to care for the general well-being of the students. One sad experience brought home to me the importance of taking the time to care. At the commencement of a new term we had a fresh intake of students, one of whom was a Year Eight boy named Belden. He had two brothers in the school, Kirschen and Cadam.

One morning I cancelled my Year Eight German class, which was also my home class, and shared my concern with the students about the poor dynamics among them. I challenged them to go to others in the class, whom they had offended or maligned, to put things right. Then I waited. One courageous girl got up and walked over to a big strapping Year Eight boy and asked him to forgive her for talking about him behind his back. He bent down and hugged her in front of everyone. This was the catalyst for the rest of the class, and for the next forty five minutes tears flowed as matters were put right and relationships were restored.

Belden was absolutely amazed at this and whispered to me that he had never seen anything like it in his life. I explained to him briefly that most of the children in the class had a relationship with Jesus, and out of that came their desire to live in good relationships with each other. He said he wanted what they had. After class, another male student and I went into my office, where Belden prayed a simple prayer and found his own faith in God.

Belden was delighted when I gave him a Gideons' New Testament, and on his return home he showed it to his younger brothers, with whom he also shared his experience. The next day during School Assembly he talked about his new found faith in front of the whole school. However, during the day he expressed his deep concern to me about his parents' marriage, which was in serious trouble. When he went home from school that day, his parents had a violent fight, and his mother decided to go and stay overnight with her sister in a distant suburb.

No-one could have foreseen the horrific events that were about to unfold in this home. His father had sinister plans, and later that night he took a gun and shot his three young sons, then poured petrol all over the house. He then put music on and phoned his wife, and said, "I have done it." She immediately knew what he meant and screamed at him on the phone, begging him to stop. In total desperation she called the emergency number to get help, but it was too late. Before they could reach him, the father set fire to the house and then shot himself. When the police and fire brigade arrived at the scene they pulled the three boys out of the burning house, but Belden was the only one who, although severely injured, was still alive. He lived until the following day, but died at exactly the same time as the school community released him to God in prayer.

Our pastor ministered to the boys' mother and prayed with her for comfort and strength during this tragic time. Student representatives from each of the boys' classes attended the funeral, and almost every one of their classmates wrote a letter to the mother, who had to go through the awful trauma of facing those four coffins – her whole family destroyed in one terrible night. This incident had a lasting impact on the school community and brought about a time of deep reflection and renewed faith among the children as they realised just how precious life is.

In 1983 my Dad died. Pippa and I flew to Koblenz to arrange the funeral. I was not sure of his salvation, and this caused me deep heartache. In my last telephone conversation with him I had assured him that God would look after him and that everything would be all right. But he passed away after what should have been a routine operation and his death was a shock to the medical staff, let alone to Mum and to me. Mum insisted that she wanted to see him again and so I accompanied her. When I saw his face I was shocked. Unbeknown to me his body had been the subject of an autopsy to determine the cause of death and this had affected his facial muscles. I was beside myself.

After we flew back to Australia Malcolm prayed with me and I had a wonderful vision (I have them rarely). I revisited my father, and this time the cool room was not grey and stark, but full of angels who brightened the room and filled it with light. On the other side of the coffin stood Jesus. He took my hand and my father's in His, comforting me with a face full of mercy and compassion. Then, indicating that it was time to go, He took my dear Dad away with Him. I have been at peace ever since. Out of the blue years later, a friend turned to me over dinner and said, "Both your parents are with the Lord." This was such a confirmation to me and brought great comfort.

TIME FOR CHANGE

In 1993 I took six month's long service leave and accompanied Malcolm to Germany, where the Lord made it clear to me that I was to resign from my position at the school. It was a hard decision since I was passionate about teaching and loved the students and staff.

A new door of opportunity opened up for me shortly after my resignation from teaching when a friend of mine invited me to join the staff of her small business, Hire-a-Guide, which took groups of visitors on tours of popular attractions around Canberra including New Parliament House, the National Museum and Floriade. This work was very flexible and fitted in with my busy schedule as well as our trips abroad. It involved my learning Australian history, which I have grown to understand and appreciate. On the tours I met people from all over the world and enthusiastically shared with them my pride in Canberra and its heritage.

It is encouraging to know that people appreciate

the love I feel for my adopted country, and Canberra in particular. As one person wrote:

"Ingrid, your fiery and passionate enthusiasm was inspiring when I was privileged recently to experience your guided tour of new Parliament House. As you waxed lyrical over the beautiful Italian marble work in the foyer; the different types of timber used throughout the building from many of the great forests of Australia; the significance behind the Aboriginal design in the front courtyard; and the story of the magnificent tapestry hanging in the great hall, I was impressed that you had done your homework and knew all the background information which made it so interesting. I was intrigued with the story of the four beautiful tapestries displaying Australian flora and fauna, designed and fabricated by school children with learning difficulties, which you felt typified the Australian psyche of giving everyone a go, of which you were very proud. We felt caught up with you into the human stories and historical background of the various items on display such as the Magna Carta, and the portraits of each of the prime ministers since Federation. History came alive as you drew us into the story of the functioning of the parliament in the upper and lower houses, the design of the building and the treasures it contained. We came away with a new appreciation of the history of parliament and this magnificent and unique building, and were thankful that we had enjoyed it with such an enthusiastic guide."

OVERSEAS EXPERIENCES

Malcolm has worked extremely hard and has been greatly blessed in his job. He was promoted to a professorship in 2004. His field is the historical linguistics of the Pacific and this has involved invitations to conferences and institutions in many countries, including Germany, France, the USA, Taiwan, Japan and the UK. We feel that we should go together on these trips because the Lord always seems to open doors of opportunity for us to minister together.

During a stay in Taiwan in 2003 we ran an Alpha Course (a video series of basic studies on Christianity) in Taipei, through which we made new friends. We returned to Taiwan in 2004 and continued to share our faith and build relationships with these friends. On one visit I was invited to preach in a little indigenous church where the majority of the people spoke Mandarin, the pastor spoke a little English, and the tribes-people spoke the local indigenous language. A Taiwanese friend translated most effectively and we were able to pray for people afterwards. That was a precious time indeed, and I felt very privileged. Our hearts are very drawn towards Taiwan.

In 2005, from April to July, Malcolm was given a visiting Fellowship at St. Catherine's in Oxford in the UK. This happened through the good offices of our generous friend J.C. Smith, a lecturer at the College and also an expert guide to the joys of life in Oxford. During the four months Malcolm wrote six papers and gave five talks. We were provided with a beautiful flat in North Oxford and were able to enter into the exciting life of the college. I loved 'high table' on Fridays. The food was exceptional cordon bleu cuisine, prepared by a chef trained at the Dorchester.

It was inspirational to meet people who had been teaching all their lives, and who, although getting on in years, still felt that they had much to give. Professor Michael Sullivan, who lived above us, had been a Professor of Modern Chinese Art at Oxford. At eighty nine years of age he was still enjoying teaching, had students coming to him every day, and was about to take his first flying lesson! Twice each year he travelled to China. His passion and vigour for life were amazing. There were at least four or five similarly inspiring people we met while at St Catherine's, who were all over eighty years of age, were very sharp and switched on and right up to date with all the daily news and world events. These people were extremely inspirational for me to be with, and I felt privileged to become their friend. They laughed when I told them, "You still have all your kangaroos in the top paddock!"

We also visited Paris, Oslo and Leipzig, where Malcolm gave talks and we met up with old friends. We were delighted to connect once again with Monika. I first met Monika when she attended one of a number of English courses that I ran years ago in Canberra for German students, and we have become close friends. Whenever we visit Germany Monika and her husband, Johannes, come to see us. For the previous three years they had a great desire to have children, and we had prayed over them, with them and for them. This time they came to visit us in Leipzig for three days, and it was such a delight for us to be able to share in their happiness as Monika was at the time four months pregnant and has since given birth to a healthy little girl.

Later in 2005 Malcolm received an invitation from a close friend of ours, the Vice Chancellor of the University of Technology in Lae, to return to Papua New Guinea to be an external assessor of applications for a professorial position that had not been filled for eight years. We felt that we should go as we had not been back for seven years. While we were there we caught up with Mait, our foster son, and his family. It was very important to us that we should visit them and grieve with them personally over the tragic loss of their beautiful daughter Ingrid, who had died of a rare blood disease at just fourteen years of age in January 2005. She had died singing praise songs to Jesus! She was a very sweet and extremely bright little girl. We shared a healing time with them as we prayed together. It was lovely to see the other grandchildren and catch up with their progress. We were also able to meet up with many of our old friends who were overjoyed to see us. We feel a very special bond and rapport with the people of Papua New Guinea. We had ten wonderful years there between 1972 and 1982 and came to love that spectacular country and its people.

JOY ON THE JOURNEY

Malcolm and I have now been happily married for over 40 years. God is such a good marriage broker. Malcolm is a wonderful husband: wise, sensitive, loving and full of integrity - just like my Dad.

Our son Jamie studied Cartography at the TAFE.

When the course was discontinued he tried various jobs, then decided to return to the TAFE, and graduated with a Diploma in Geographic Information Systems. He then went to Curtin University in Perth, Western Australia, where he obtained his degree in Cartography. He has settled in Perth. His work takes him to many different places, both in Australia and overseas. We are very proud of him.

Our daughter Pippa worked for a long time in the hospitality industry, then worked with children and elderly people, as well in as the retail industry. She also completed a course in make-up, which opened the door for a variety of interesting work experiences. In September 2005 she returned to the UK where she is, at the time of writing, working as an Assistant House Mistress at a boarding school in Ascot. She has been a wonderful daughter to us.

God has brought me a long way from my country of birth and those early beginnings when we lost everything. He has blessed us with a beautiful home overlooking Canberra, and with a wonderful family and community of friends. I never cease to be grateful to Him for his care, guidance and provision for our family.

I lead a very busy and fulfilled life, despite some serious health problems. I became incredibly tired during the day and often fell asleep sitting up. Eventually we discovered that I had sleep apnoea, a condition where I can stop breathing for up to 50 seconds at a time and where I can have many brain arousals in an hour at night. To alleviate this condition I have to wear a mask while I am asleep, fed by a machine that keeps my body supplied with constant air pressure. It's uncomfortable and very unattractive, but I am so thankful that Malcolm is understanding and fully supportive as he knows how important it is for my health and well-being.

A short while ago I was talking to a friend who mentioned a birthday party to which I should have received an invitation, but it did not arrive. I was devastated and felt excluded. Eventually the invitation came. It had gone to the wrong address and been returned to the sender. As I thought about my reaction to this, it led me back to my experience at High School when I had been excluded from the final examination, and the devastation I felt at the time. I decided to seek prayer counselling, and while talking about my past, I discovered that the deep hurt within my heart went even further back, to the occasion at the age of ten years when I took the entrance examination for the Grammar School and my maths paper was snatched from me by the invigilator and I was excluded from the exam. I thought I had dealt with these issues, but they had obviously hurt much more deeply than I realised. God has brought healing to my heart and set me free from the pain of rejection.

God continues to sustain and strengthen me through the difficult times, particularly when I am in constant pain with fibromyalgia and arthritis. A few years ago I was also diagnosed with atrial fibrillation, a heart condition which has seen me in hospital more than once. During one attack I had to have an anaesthetic so that the medical team could put a fibrillating pad on my heart to shock it back into its proper rhythm. I had a severe fall several years ago, when I broke my ankle badly, and this has caused problems with my leg, knees and hip. A hip replacement has helped me to walk properly again and this has given me considerable relief.

Although the constant pain is a nuisance and is very debilitating, my faith in God sustains me and enables me to minister to others who are far worse off than I. My mother was such a wonderful example of joy in the face of adversity, and she taught me to smile despite the circumstances. I remember a friend telling me that happiness is a choice. How true!

The things that stir my heart are hospitality and networking, along with a passion for sharing the good news of the gospel message of faith and hope with all I meet. I love bringing people from my church and neighbourhood together for fellowship, and gathering in and nurturing the students we have contact with at the ANU.

REFLECTIONS

As I look back over the years, I can see that the nickname my parents gave me when I was very young, 'Peace Child,' has acquired a significance that they never dreamed of. From my German childhood at peace in the midst of the horrors of war, I have found a haven of tranquility in the country which has adopted me. But greater than this outward peace is the peace in my heart through my relationship with a heavenly Father who loves me without limit. It is this peace that I love to share with those I meet, sometimes complete strangers, both in Australia and overseas. I have an e-mail list of over 200 friends all over the world. I pray with them, minister to them and write in four languages: English, German, French and Pidgin. I am delighted that God is using the internet for His glory to spread His gospel of peace throughout the world!

Each day of our life is a gift, and as long as my eyes open I'll focus on the new day and all the happy memories I've stored away, just for this time in my life. I read a beautiful story which said that old age is like a bank account: you withdraw from what you've put in.

The verse at my confirmation and at our wedding was Romans 8:38 and it has held its truth in my life to this day: *"For I am convinced that neither death nor life, neither angels nor demons, neither the present nor the future, nor any powers, neither height nor depth, nor anything else in all creation will be able to separate us from the love of God which is in Christ Jesus our Lord."* (NIV)

We don't know what the future holds but God has it in His hands. God has been my gracious, loving Father, and my wonderful Friend. I literally owe Him my life over and over again and want to thank Him for who He is and for how He has loved me.

Ingrid with her parents during World War II.

Ingrid and Malcolm on their wedding day in Koblenz, 1965.

Ingrid and Malcolm with Pippa and Jamie in P.N.G.

Ingrid, centre of picture, outside her home in Goroka,
PNG, with students from the Teacher's College.

Ingrid and Malcolm with a group of ANU students and friends celebrating Chinese New Year in Canberra, January 2005.

Ingrid and Malcolm celebrating their 40th wedding anniversary, 2005.

BETTY HOCKING

I first met Betty shortly after my arrival in Canberra when I was confined to bed with the flu and feeling sick, lonely and miserable. She arrived on my doorstep with a cheerful greeting and a large pot of tasty chicken soup, which warmed my heart as well as my stomach. This was typical of Betty. She is a woman of action. A doer of deeds.

Adopted herself as a child, Betty's home was always open to welfare youngsters and single mothers, including people with problems of all kinds. At one time, in the space of two years their family grew from two to six children – with four under four years of age.

Betty genuinely believes the best of people – which, as her story reveals, has sometimes led to encounters with interesting characters.

Betty is outspoken and forthright, but her words are seasoned with grace. Betty's wise counsel and practical common sense are always helpful in a crisis. She has been active in fighting for victims of injustice, and worked tirelessly for Lindy Chamberlain's acquittal. In retirement she is still championing causes for those who cannot fight for themselves.

Little Brown Duck – Canterbury Park, October 1989

She is there most nights
At dusk – alone
on the lagoon
crowded with water lilies
Bobbing and diving
Like a tiny submarine
with periscope extended

She seems less than half
the size of other ducks
who fly in pairs
Squadrons of four
line up against
my little brown duck
like chessmen – Checkmate!
Get out of here!

At sunset they depart
and she is left alone
one of a kind
Where has she come from?
Why does she stay?
Has she no-one to love her?
No home?

My heart aches
as I watch
night shadows enfold her

She reminds me of
too many people I know.

Betty Hocking

Little Girl Lost

BETTY'S STORY

The headmaster put his arm around my waist and stroked my face. "I'm lonely, Betty," he said. "Do you know, nobody cuddles me at home?"

I didn't get any cuddles at home either. In my eleven-year-old ignorance I thought that was how life was. It was gratifying to be singled out to stay back for extra help after school, and have kind words spoken to me by such an exalted person. However, although I knew nothing about sex, when his hands began to wander in places I had strict instructions not to touch, I became wary and confused. I made excuses to avoid him, and eventually he found another little girl who needed 'help'. The lesson he had taught me was not to trust.

In the poem I wrote in October 1989 I identified with the little brown duck. All my life I never quite seemed to belong.

****

I grew up in the small country town of Laura, in the wheat belt north of Adelaide, South Australia, in a home where there was a lot of discord. My adoptive father Ben was a generous, outgoing man, but the depression years were not easy times. Some of the conflict in our home may have been due to his tendency to help others when his own family was in need. He also suffered from nightmares as a result of his service in World War I. We were horrified by the story my adoptive mother Lurlie told of waking one night to find his hands around her neck trying to strangle her, mistaking her for the enemy. Fortunately for her, she was able to wake him from his dream. The effects of war do not end with the armistice.

My adoptive mother Lurlie was a difficult, unpredictable woman. I can only remember once experiencing her arms around me in love rather than in punishment, and that was the evening I was badly frightened by a neighbour's practical joke. Although I was terrified by what I thought was a snake crawling up my leg, it was worth it for the comforting I received.

FINDING MY FAMILY

I had no problems setting off for my first day at school. I was excited and had looked forward to it for months. However, school held unexpected revelations for me.

At morning recess three little girls older than I came up to me and said, "Hello, Betty. Do you know who we are?" I had not the vaguest idea, but they proceeded to tell me. "We are Winifred, Daphne and Gertie, and we are your sisters." At that point another girl named Mary joined us. "She is not your sister. She is my sister," she declared. Was this some sort of a joke? I knew I had a brother, Ian, who was fourteen months younger than me and who was still at home with mother Lurlie as he had not yet started school. Why were these girls so keen to claim me as their sister?

Winifred, the eldest of the three, explained that my mother (and theirs) had died when I was a baby of six months. The school bell rang, and we resumed classes before I had a chance to digest this information. At lunch time I caught up on more of the story, which the girls were eager to impart to me. They explained to me that there were eight other children besides me, and that after the death of our mother our father could not manage us all alone, even with the help of the two eldest girls, Elsie and Nell, who were barely in their teens. Two boys and a girl had been placed in a children's home in Adelaide for three years, but they were now back with the family. Daphne had remained at home, and Gertie was still living on a farm with friends.

Because I was so young, I had been adopted by the family I thought were my own. This had been against the wishes of my eldest sister, and she carried a burden of guilt all her life for not having been able to keep the family together. The reason Mary thought I was her sister was because her mother had cared for me for a time before ill health forced her to pass me on to someone else.

I was full of questions when I went home from school that afternoon. "Mummy, I met some girls at school who say they are my sisters."

"You keep away from them!" she replied.

I was shocked by her angry reaction. But angry reactions from Mummy were not a new experience.

When I asked why, she responded, "You just do as I say, that's all. It's true that they didn't want you so they gave you to us, but you are not to have anything to do with them. If I hear of you speaking to them again, there'll be trouble."

And trouble there was! The first year at school passed reasonably uneventfully. My sisters and I were able to get together occasionally in the school yard to guiltily exchange a little information, knowing we were disobeying orders. When my brother Ian started school the following year he reported to mother Lurlie every time he saw us speaking to one another, and I was regretfully forced to avoid my sisters. In a country school of less than one hundred pupils it was impossible to keep secrets.

Over the years I gradually pieced together the full story. My father migrated to Australia from London, married my mother in Adelaide, and tried to settle on the land. Like many Englishmen, he understood little of farming in Australia, and with the added burden of losing his wife within months of my birth, he left the farm and moved with his eight children into the small country town of Laura. His eldest son was barely fifteen, and the oldest daughter just turned fourteen. He had no-one else to help and pleaded with his mother in England to come and join him in Australia. However, his father refused to face the long sea journey.

My adoptive family was very different from the one into which I had been born, and because both families continued to live in the same small country town of Laura, life was not easy. I later learnt that my adoptive parents' marriage, even at that early stage, was difficult. They thought they were unable to have children, but they did have a son just over a year after they adopted me. Apparently father Ben had pleaded with my natural father to sign the adoption papers, because he hoped a baby might improve their relationship.

I often tried to imagine what my real mother would have been like and how different life might have been had she lived, but I had little to go on – not even a photograph. I dreamed once of being held in her arms. It seemed more real than a dream, and it happened one night when I was particularly upset. Perhaps it was a subconscious memory. I tried to hold on to it, but when I looked into her face misty clouds drifted between us and I was disappointed that I could not see her features or carry the experience back with me into reality.

I loved school. It was an escape from the tensions at home and the emotional problems of mother Lurlie. There was always great excitement when the circus came to town. We were given the morning off from school to watch the animals unloaded from the train. The pay-off came when we had to write an essay about it for homework. I loved to wander over to the circus and absorb the sights and sounds. Once I brought a young girl whose parents worked in the circus home to play. That was not regarded favourably. "You are the biggest collector of lame dogs I have ever seen," mother Lurlie said.

We never owned a motor car, although at one stage early in my life I remember father Ben owning a motor cycle and side-car. For years I had nightmares that involved being hunted down by a motor bike, and once I asked if there had been any incident which might have given rise to those persistent dreams. I was assured there was not. Perhaps they were rather as a result of the white gander chasing me around the garden on my tricycle when I was two. In the depression years even bicycles were beyond our reach for a long time. Television was unheard of. We did not have radios, which were still quite new. I remember being very excited when I visited some family friends who had a crystal set, and I was able to listen to crackly music from a radio station in Port Pirie, all of thirty miles away!

Sometimes in summer we had heavy dust storms. The sky would grow dark, and the dust swirled down from the north in thick red-brown clouds that covered everything with grit. We would shut all the doors and windows and pull down the holland blinds, but even so it took days to get that red dust out of the house after the storm had passed.

Because our water supply came from two large galvanized iron tanks, filled by drainage from the roof of the house and the large corrugated iron shed in the back yard, we could not have lawns, but father Ben and mother Lurlie, with unenthusiastic assistance from Ian and I, kept the garden beds weed-less and the paths scraped clean. Every bucket of waste water was saved for the garden. In drought years we had to buy bore water to see us through. It was heavily mineralised, and the soap formed a scum when we bathed in it. Fortunately we always had enough rain water to drink. The bore water had a terrible taste.

Ian and I eventually acquired bikes, put together by father Ben from bits and pieces given to him by friends. These were useful for our delivery service for parcels of dry cleaning wrapped in brown paper and tied with string from our parents' dry cleaning business. We enjoyed our bikes, often riding long distances with friends at weekends to other little townships, or just out into the country to explore.

ESCAPE

From time to time most children entertain ideas about running away from home. When I was nine I was unhappy with all the discord at home, and even tried on one occasion, unsuccessfully of course, to smother myself with pillows. It was then that I hit on the idea of returning to my own family.

One morning just before dawn, I packed up a few treasures with my school books in a sugar bag, wrote a note explaining where I was going, and slipped out of the house. There was a light frost and the air was crisp and clear. It was quite a walk to the other end of the town where my father lived with his second wife Alice, their daughters Alice and Mathina, and the youngest of my sisters, Daphne and Gertie. When I arrived it was still early and no-one was stirring. I did not have the courage to go and knock on the door so I was at a loss as to what I should do. My father's wife Alice saw me peeping from behind a rusty sheet of corrugated iron near the gatepost and drew my father's attention to my presence there.

He came over and took me by the hand. He was a tall man, thin and a little stooped. I had seen him once or twice in the main street when I went to the post office to collect the mail. Meeting at the post office was a focal point for people to pass the time of day, but I usually looked the other way because I was forbidden to speak to him. This morning he was very surprised to see me at his gate. "Betty! What are you doing here?" he gently asked. "I'm unhappy, and I've come home," I replied.

We walked into the kitchen, where my father took me on his knee and showed me a photograph. "That is a picture of your mother," he said. "I want you to know that I love you. The children and I did not want to give you up, but the family you are with were very insistent on those adoption papers being signed if they were to keep you, and I didn't know what else to do." That at least sounded better than what I had been told – that they did not want me, so had given me away. "I would love to keep you here now," my father continued, "but the law forbids it. Those adoption papers mean I have to send you back home."

So – I had gone through all this for nothing! I knew there would be a heavy price to pay at the other end, but what could I do? What power has a child in a world run for the convenience of grown ups?

My father loaded us all into his buckboard utility just as the local police constable arrived. My note had been found and no time wasted in taking what was considered to be appropriate action. The policeman stood on the running board of the car while we drove back to Samuel Street. I was mortified to be under police protection and silently prayed that no-one would see what was happening. Mother Lurlie and father Ben were all grateful smiles and thank you's while the constable was around. "Thank you for bringing her back constable," mother Lurlie said, ignoring my natural father. "I'd give my life for that child."

When the others had left and father Ben had gone to work, I received a beating for my troubles, including being swung around the room by my hair and having my face slammed into the mirror. Eventually the beating finished and mother Lurlie took away my books and my watch (a Christmas present), until she calmed down some weeks later and I gradually got them back. I did not try to run away again, though I often stood by the front fence at day's end and imagined walking into the setting sun.

****

It was not all bad. We had some good times, but they generally involved other people. One such occasion was at Christmas when the farmers from the Lutheran church would sometimes invite Ian and me to the Christmas Eve children's service. We loved the big Christmas tree with its lighted candles, the hearty singing of the Christmas carols, and the deep throated tones of the pedal organ. At the end of the evening there was always a bag of coloured popcorn or sweets to take home. I also enjoyed attending Sunday School at the local Anglican church and talking with the elderly rector, Father North, who told me I was a princess because I was a daughter of God, our Heavenly King.

Sometimes we would stay overnight at friends' homes or go on visits to farms, where we enjoyed the activities and hard work of farm life, including hay making, milking cows, bread making and horse riding. Unfortunately it was always a one-sided arrangement, as I was not allowed to have friends to come and stay at my home. I loved one farm in particular, where there were children both slightly older and younger than I, and would have traded life in the town for life on that farm at any price.

WAR

With the advent of World War II in September 1939, air raid shelters became the vogue. Trenches were dug at the schools, and air raid drill was regularly held. We all had our special instructions, and when the siren sounded we had to march in orderly fashion to our places in the trenches, much to the delight of those who liked an excuse for a break from lessons! There was always a shadow over these occasions because a friend's father had died of a heart attack while helping to dig the trenches.

Father Ben constructed a beautiful underground air raid shelter in our back yard. It had sandbags and a properly camouflaged dirt roof covering heavy logs, and we were very proud of it. It was also cool on a hot day and a great place to play. It became a well-used cubby house. Fortunately that was its only function and we never had to use it for its intended purpose. Before he left to join the army father Ben taught us how to use a rifle and issued us with ration packs and instructions to head for the bush if the Japanese invaded. Now nightmares of hiding from enemy bombers replaced the earlier dreams of pursuit by motor bikes.

My friends and I worked hard for the Schools Patriotic Fund collecting metal, newspapers, bottles and old rags for recycling. We were rewarded with blue and gold badges and little achievement bars to attach to them. Competition was keen, and we wore our badges and bars with pride. At weekends we picked olives, which grew wild in trees around the town. These were sent to the city to make olive oil and gained us further points for the war effort.

The war had its frightening moments for us, but it was much more remote than in these present days when every act of death and destruction is portrayed in colour on our television screens in our living rooms. There were exciting moments, such as when an armoured tank division came thundering through the main street on its way north and we collected autographs from the drivers. I rather hoped that the war might last until I was old enough to join one of the

Women's Services. Fortunately it did not.

By this time I was travelling each day to Gladstone High School, fourteen kilometres away. We had to travel in a bus which, as I remember it now, must surely have been home made! It was square and wooden, painted red, with long, narrow black vinyl seats and wooden sections that folded down at the end of the rows once everyone was on board. The trick was to get in fast enough so that you could slide across to the window seat on the other side. The last ones in got the uncomfortable wooden seats and had to move to let out the students who were dropped at wayside stops. We had great times on that old bus as we sang with gusto all the popular war time songs of the day, such as Lily Marlene. We knew them all.

My interest in putting ideas on paper began at an early age, when, with the help of three girls who lived next door, we produced our own 'newspaper' on pages torn from old school books, including drawings, verses, and stories – even a serial that ran for several issues. I had numerous pen friends throughout Australia and overseas. These helped to fill what appears to have been a need to write and communicate. Pen pals and essay writing took the place of an earlier phase when I had an imaginary friend, based on the Phantom, in a serial which ran for many years in the Australian Women's Mirror. Over the years I won a number of prizes in essay writing competitions for newspapers and magazines. I also wrote other poems and put them all together in a booklet. I wish I had that now. None of my treasures survived mother Lurlie's zest for tidiness. An earlier composition written in primary school was a fourteen page essay on life on the moon as I imagined it to be. It gained a 99% mark, and was read aloud to the class.

Father Ben had been in the Light Horse Brigade in the Middle East in World War I, and there were trophies from Egypt and photographs, as well as a pastel reproduction of him in army uniform that hung on the living room wall. When World War II was declared he lost no time in enlisting in a Garrison Battalion. He came home on leave in uniform once or twice and Ian and I were very proud of him. The house was much more peaceful without the constant arguing between our parents. No longer were we woken at night by the frightening sounds of their verbal and physical battles.

In June 1942 something went wrong with a smallpox vaccination given to father Ben. He had a long spell in hospital in Adelaide, during which time he slowly became more paralysed, and eventually died. Mother Lurlie spent some months in Adelaide, but Ian and I were not allowed to visit him. We stayed most of that time with friends on our favourite farm about three miles out in the country, or with an aunt who lived in the town.

Sadly, because he had been away from home and we knew his condition was gradually worsening, the inevitability of father Ben's death became just another difficulty we had to face and there was no real shock at his passing. An incident involving death that caused me more trauma was when my uncle insisted that I drown in a kerosene tin the families of kittens which had multiplied in mother Lurlie's absence, while he disposed of the mother cats. If I remember correctly we had accumulated seventeen cats and kittens from those that were regularly dumped in the church yard nearby.

I cannot remember a time when we did not regard ourselves as poor and money was not scarce. In late 1942 one of my two eldest sisters, Nell, turned up at our house. I was sent away from the front verandah where she was talking with mother Lurlie, but I managed to linger close enough to catch part of the conversation. It appeared that one of my three brothers, Frank, had been killed in action at El Alemein, and his will contained a small legacy for me. Neither Nell nor mother Lurlie were at ease with one another. The conversation was polite, but very strained. It was not a large amount, I think about five pounds ($10), but it was never mentioned again. However it meant a lot to me to know that my brother, whom I had never met, had included me in his will, even if I had to eavesdrop to find out about it.

Within a few months there was a third death in my family circle. Shortly after father Ben's death I was told in an offhand way by mother Lurlie that my natural father had died of a sudden heart attack. He had a weak heart, they said, as a result of mustard gas attacks in the First World War. If I felt any emotion at this news I quickly stifled it. Mother Lurlie had been easier to live with since father Ben was no longer around and I did not want to give her any grounds for a tirade of criticism against my family. I merely shrugged and turned away. My father had told me he loved me, and held me in his arms – once. That was a memory I was keeping to myself. It was all I had.

The last year I lived in Laura was, as I remember, the best. My brother Ian was not living at home. He spent an extended period on the farm after father Ben's death. Upon leaving school he worked as an apprentice mechanic at a local garage and joined the RAAF as soon as he was old enough. In the winter mother Lurlie and I lit the wood fire in the grate in her bedroom instead of the living room to save wood and the work of cleaning out another grate, and sat in cane lounge chairs knitting, embroidering or reading until it was time for bed. It was cosy, and the nearest we ever came to comradeship with one another. It was as though I had reached an age where I was no longer in any way a burden or a threat. My childhood was over, and I was glad.

NEW HORIZONS

I completed high school in 1943, obtaining the Leaving Certificate. The next step was either further education in Adelaide, or to obtain a job.

I moved to Adelaide and lived with mother Lurlie's second sister and mother while I completed my studies. I had my heart set on training to become a teacher, which would have been financed by Legacy, an organisation that takes care of War Widows and their children. However, mother Lurlie insisted that I go to business college instead. "You'll never make it through teachers' college," she said, embarrassing me in front of the Legacy Officer. "I had enough trouble with your nerves getting you through the Leaving Examination."

In reality my nervousness was not due to too much study, which I greatly enjoyed, but to living in the uncertainty of mother Lurlie's unpredictable temper. It took me a long time to forgive mother Lurlie for that interference in my future. It was not until I entered teaching through the back door at the Reid Technical College, as it was then known, many years later as a commercial teacher in Canberra that I felt the obstacle which had been put in my way was at least partly overcome.

In the meantime though, I was enrolled in 'Miss Mann's Business College,' a private commercial college in Pirie Street, Adelaide. I found the course well within my capacity and was soon employed assisting in the night-time commercial classes. However, my rural carelessness of speech proved to be too much for the genteel Miss Mann, and my employment was politely terminated when I was overheard showing a student a particular shorthand outline and informing her blithely that it went "way up the page to billy-oh!"

After completing the commercial college course I obtained a full-time position as typist/telephonist at the Repatriation Commission in Adelaide, and at the end of the year sat for the Public Service Entrance

Examination. I came second in the State of South Australia and was offered a posting as a shorthand typist in Canberra, Darwin or Alice Springs. There were some doubts expressed by mother Lurlie and aunt Bessie about the wisdom of my moving so far away from their influence, but nothing was done to prevent me from going. Because I was only sixteen, it was officially decided by the Public Service Board that I should go to Canberra. It did not matter to me that the decision was taken out of my hands – it was all new and part of life's great adventure.

Because it was still war time and food rationing and blackout curtains were part of our lives, travelling by train to Canberra required a great deal of form filling and bureaucratic red tape, but eventually all was in order. I had some enjoyable times during that year in Adelaide, but I had no regrets at moving on. There were no close relationships to hold me, and I had no real home.

Canberra in 1944 was little more than a large country town with a population of around 20,000, most of them public servants. When I arrived I was appointed to the Department of Post War Reconstruction and assigned accommodation in Hotel Ainslie, which had been taken over as a girls' hostel. The weekly tariff of thirty six shillings was considered expensive. Gorman House, just down the road, charged only thirty shillings!

The Department was housed in the old fibro and weatherboard hospital buildings, which later became part of the Australian National University at Acton. Lucerne paddocks occupied much of the area now covered by the waters of Lake Burley Griffin. Petrol was rationed, and cars were scarce as a result of the war. My friends and I rode bicycles to work, and for pleasure to the Cotter Reserve, Coppins Crossing, Kambah Pool and other spots along the Murrumbidgee River.

I made some half-hearted attempts to become involved in a youth group at St John's Church of England in Reid at the invitation of my friend Mary Dale, but somehow it did not compare well with the other entertainment available. However, I liked the historic old stone church and often went to services there. Although baptized as an infant in the Anglican Church in Laura, I had not been confirmed, so I joined a confirmation class to prepare for this event. I did not manage to attend many classes because of heavy work commitments, but I was confirmed anyway. It was a ritual I did not really understand. However, I was now able to take the communion wafer and the wine, which gave me a feeling of 'belonging' somewhere at last – in the Anglican church.

The Albert Hall was the principal centre of live entertainment, with the Capitol Theatre at Manuka providing the celluloid variety. I had not been in Canberra long when we celebrated the end of the war. There was a morning service at the War Memorial, in walking distance of the hostel. In the evening we made our way to the Albert Hall. The victory celebrations went on all night, with thousands of Canberrans singing, dancing and generally letting off steam. It was a wonderful feeling of release to know that the war was over at last.

One of our favourite places for outings was the Manuka Services Hut. Meals were served, and dances held, primarily for the benefit of servicemen on leave. Volunteers were always needed to help serve the meals and wash the dishes, and 'Friday night at the Rec Hut' was a regular end-of-week activity for many of us. There were also Saturday night dances at the Albert Hall and the Causeway Hall. These were all acceptable meetings places for young people.

Commonwealth Bridge at that time was a rough wooden structure spanning the Molonglo River. Sometimes, my room mate Lilian and I rode our bikes home in the early morning hours after visiting friends and, with the river dark and mysterious below us, we would be wrapped in a cold blanket of fog while we pedalled furiously to reach City Hill on the other side of the rattling bridge.

Hostel residents spent many evenings yarning around the log fires after May 1st, the magic date when we were allowed to set light to the wood provided by the Department of the Interior. Rigid rules demanded that no fires be lit in hostel fireplaces before May 1st, no matter how chilly the winds or heavy the frosts!

ROMANCE AND MARRIAGE

Morning tea breaks at the Department of Post-War

Reconstruction were taken on the verandahs in the sun and were times of lively discussions and blossoming romances. I became aware of the special interest of Jim Hocking, a research officer in the Regional Planning Section, in getting me to do his work. Soon I became a regular visitor in that Section for morning tea. In the warmer weather we would all sit on the edge of the old hospital wooden verandah and discuss everything from politics to the latest repertory show. I found these discussions much more stimulating than those in the Typing Pool.

The next step was not far away. The thirty three year old civil engineer from Melbourne asked for a date with the seventeen year old steno and, Canberra being what it was, everyone in the Department and the Hostel knew about it by nine o'clock the following morning. After a brief courtship Jim proposed to me under the pine trees near the back door of the Hotel Ainslie. Although I was greatly attracted to him, there was some heart searching necessary before I felt I could give him an answer. I did not receive any helpful advice from mother Lurlie when I visited her to seek her opinion about this most important decision of my life. She was favourably impressed with Jim, but not with the idea of marriage as an institution. Her comment was, "Marriages are supposed to be made in heaven, but in my experience they are made in hell."

At the time I did not understand why Jim, a quietly spoken, older, ex-army officer attracted me more than others had done. I later realised it was partly because he introduced me to a world for which I had an instinctive yearning: the world of classical music, theatre and philosophical discussion. The younger men in my life, although possessing many likeable qualities, were cast in a more practical mould. Jim was the only person who had ever reached past the defences I had built up for protection over the years and drew me out of myself.

I decided to accept his proposal and to make the engagement official in March, when I turned eighteen. In July of that same year, 1946, we were married in the historic old church of St John the Baptist. I wore a dress borrowed from a friend, and a work colleague stepped into the role of bridesmaid. Friends arranged a small reception in their home after the service, and the best man provided transport in his own car to the Blue Mountains for our honeymoon, as the trains were not running due to a coal strike. Neither Jim's widowed mother, Mabel, nor mother Lurlie attended the wedding ceremony. They felt that the effort and expense of the long trip, one from Melbourne, the other from Laura, for the brief ceremony was not warranted, and promised to come and see us when we had a house and had settled down. Until they became too frail to travel, they visited on average once a year, at different times. In spite of a few hiccups we managed to maintain a good relationship with both of them.

I had been a guest at the Hotel Ainslie just long enough to become eligible for a single room, and when friends from the hostel helped me to dress for the wedding, I had only one regret. I had longed for a room to myself all my life. I had shared a bedroom with my brother, my aunt, my cousin and other girls, and had such a short time in which to enjoy the luxury of a room of my own. It was to be a long time before I had that privilege again.

We moved from the hostel into a rented government house in Turner, which we later bought for $18,000. All the houses were on large blocks in an area regarded as being out of town.

When Jim married me I imagine he had no idea of just what he had taken on. I looked innocent, and I was. Perhaps I also seemed to be a country girl who would find home-making and raising a family an entirely satisfying career, and I wasn't!

Someone has said that equality means being free to choose what you really want to do. Over the years Jim adapted to some unconventional situations as he endorsed equality and gave me free rein to do the things I either wanted to do, or felt I should do. How much of this was due to a subconscious fear of losing me, I am unsure. He had previously been engaged to a girl who changed her mind a few days prior to the wedding. Comments he made occasionally seemed to indicate a baseless anxiety that I, too, might one day bring our relationship to a sudden end.

Babies soon arrived in most of the homes around us. Ours was blessed with the birth of two beautiful daughters, Lesley in 1948, and Claire in 1951. We visited, and became friends, with many couples, knowing by name all that lived nearby. We cooked on green and cream enamelled wood-burning Canberra stoves. Washing day meant lighting up the wood copper to boil the whites. The bathroom was well heated, summer and winter, by the chip bath heater. Open fireplaces in lounge and dining rooms made cleaning out the ashes a daily winter chore and filtered fine dust throughout the house. It needed a ton of hand chopped wood a month in winter to cope with the fuel needs.

A shopping trip to Civic could take me considerably longer than expected, not only because of the infrequent bus service, but because I encountered so many friends and would stop to chat under the colonnades, the only buildings housing shops at that time. There was ample free parking for those who owned cars and whose husbands were prepared to walk, cycle or bus to work. Queanbeyan and Goulburn however, were regarded as superior shopping centres, and the frugal made regular expeditions out of town to stock up on groceries and other items. Holiday trips to the coast were somewhat hazardous on the gravel road over the Clyde Mountain to Bateman's Bay.

In 1955 Jim was granted twelve months long service leave from the Public Service and we took Lesley and Claire with us for a world adventure trip, travelling by ocean liner and train. We bought a small Ford van for our expeditions in Europe and the British Isles. It was an exciting year, but is a full story on its own.

RETURN TO ROOTS

In 1959 I received a letter from my eldest sister Elsie telling me of the arrangements for her only daughter's wedding in January 1960. It was planned to have a guard of honour of all Marjorie's girl cousins at the wedding and Elsie and her husband were hopeful that we might consider coming to Whyalla, South Australia, with our two daughters for this special occasion. We wrote to mother Lurlie, who was still living in Laura, telling her of our proposed trip and our desire to visit her on the way. In her reply she expressed her strong disapproval of our plan, which she did not sanction. We decided to go anyway, and made the trip towing our new Viscount caravan, a method of holidaying we enjoyed for many years to come. On the way we visited my sister Winifred and her family in Barmera, South Australia, and met my sister Nell and her husband at Crystal Brook for afternoon tea, so the children had two brief encounters with family members before they were swamped with relatives at Whyalla. To avoid arguments we by-passed Laura and mother Lurlie, and travelled via the coast road through Port Pirie to Whyalla.

It was an historic family occasion. All my blood brothers and sisters, except Frank, were there. Our girls had a unique opportunity to meet unknown aunts, uncles and cousins. On looking back, the wedding in Whyalla was a remarkable time. I not only met brothers and sisters, some of whom I had no previous contact with at all, but when I also learned many unknown things about my own past. In spite of my different upbringing, it was fascinating to see that there were mannerisms and attitudes which we held in common.

Though we can never recapture the lost years, there is immeasurable satisfaction in knowing one's roots and catching up with blood relatives that should not be denied to adopted children. I like to think our parents in Heaven rejoiced with us in Whyalla on January 9, 1960, knowing that the little girl who was lost had come home at last.

My adoptive brother Ian and I did not communicate or see much of each other after he left home and joined the Air Force. He eventually married and lived in Melbourne with his wife and three children. When the marriage failed he moved to Townsville, where he settled permanently.

Both Ian and I contributed financially to mother Lurlie's needs from our salaries before our marriages. Imagine our disappointment when, after she passed away, we discovered that she had ignored both of us in her will, and had left a substantial sum of money to an Adelaide home for abandoned cats! This had the positive effect of bringing Ian and me together again as we joined forces to contest the will and managed to obtain a portion of what was rightfully ours. I visited him in North Queensland, and in 2006 helped arrange his transfer to Victoria to be closer to his daughters when he was no longer able to manage his large house and garden.

EXTENDED FAMILY

Wanting more children, who did not come along as planned, I filled up the house with welfare youngsters and single mothers, including people with problems of all kinds. Officially, because we already had two children, we were not considered eligible to adopt. However, solicitors and ministers of churches were often approached privately by mothers-to-be, and maintained lists of would-be parents who were approved by the Child Welfare Department.

To our delight, in January 1961 Helen came to us through the Anglican church. Nine days old, she was a chubby little bundle with blonde hair so fine it could scarcely be seen. When Helen was 14 months old, in March 1962, I was rung by a solicitor and told that a three week old baby boy was available for adoption and that I could pick him up that day. I rang Jim at work to say that, if he agreed, I could collect our son immediately. He was getting used to surprises. "Very well," he answered, "but after this will you please make sure our name comes off all lists!" And so Geoff, with his dark hair and olive skin, joined our family.

In June of that same year, we were contacted by a Welfare Officer and asked if we could temporarily take into our care two emotionally disturbed German speaking toddlers from a migrant background. Their mother's mental health had broken down with the stress of raising too many children under sub-standard living conditions. Since one of the boys had previously lived with us for six months and had settled down very well, they wanted to know if we could please take that same little boy, and also his older brother, because they did not want to separate them. I explained that we had just adopted a second baby and I already had two in nappies, and suggested they first look for other foster parents for the children. It was wasted breath. A few days later the officials were on the doorstep with a case of clothes and Bruno (Bruce) two and a half, and Wilhelm (Billy) three and a half. They lived with us for over twelve years. So in the space of two years our family grew from two to six children – with four under four years of age!

Over the years there were also a number of welfare children who needed homes. One of these was Rose, who joined us at age eleven and stayed for two years, a special child. Her sister, Gwenny, was quite different. She was fourteen when the Welfare Department asked us to take her in. When she disappeared one night and came home on the garbage truck next morning I decided teenagers were probably outside my area of expertise.

We gave temporary refuge to sons and daughters of friends from time to time. Only in recent years did I discover that one of these had taken advantage of my naivety. The tomato plants that I diligently watered for him at his request while he went away for a week were, I learned much later, of the smokeable variety, and probably could have gained me, at the least, a hefty fine!

SPIRITUAL AWAKENING

In 1962, not long after we adopted Geoff, a friend took me to my first Charismatic church meeting. Although I had been raised in the Anglican tradition, and held a strong belief in God, I found the concept of actually experiencing His presence in a tangible way and getting to know Him like a close friend was something new and exciting. When I agreed to be baptized by immersion, and came up out of the baptismal water speaking in a prayer language I had never heard before (described in the Bible in Mark 16:16-18 and Acts 2:4 as being filled with the Spirit), a whole new world opened up for me. The foundational Biblical truths that are basic to all Christian churches took on a whole new meaning as I experienced the power of God that brought these truths to life.

There were some traumatic as well as ecstatic experiences to be faced along the way, but from that day to this (over 40 years later) my life and that of my family has been guided and influenced by the reality of God's presence and love.

****

Somewhere in between all of these experiences, with a friend, I established and ran Canberra's first secretarial agency, which we named 'Secretarial Club and Typing Service,' and as a result worked in a number of interesting part-time and temporary jobs, which included as a hansard typist at Parliament House and reporting the local Advisory Council meetings. The latter involved speed shorthand taking of minutes, which I later typed up at home with my young children playing around my feet. I also taught commercial subjects at the local TAFE (Technical and Further Education) College and, at one stage, had an early morning, and I mean early – 4 am, bread run to help with pocket money for Bruce and Billy. I can remember thinking as I dragged my reluctant body out of bed on a cold winter's morning yet again, that this was about the craziest idea in a lifetime of crazy ideas!

Lesley and Claire attended the Church of England Girls' Grammar School in Forrest, and made steady progress in spite of the ever increasing family. Both were kept busy with music and church activities.

ANGELA

One morning, as I was driving home through the lucerne paddocks where the peaceful waters of Lake Burley Griffin now rest, I spotted a lonely, dejected little figure trudging along beside the road. Touched by her forlorn appearance, I stopped and offered her a lift. She climbed into our Kombi van and promptly burst into tears. "I am in big trouble," she sobbed in broken English. "I have just lost job. I have nowhere to go but back to hospital and doctor tell he puts me in Goulburn mental home and I never get out if I don't keep job."

My brain worked overtime. "Well, you can come home with me if you like," I said, picturing in my mind the small caravan we had under a carport at the back of the house.

The tears stopped flowing, and her face lit up. "Can I? I will have to go first to hospital to pick up some things."

Silently praying and believing for God's provision, I answered the Almoner's questions with confidence.

"Who are you?"

"A friend."

"Do you have a job for her to go to?"

"No, but I will have."

Angela's story began in northern Italy. At the end of World War II, because of the ongoing struggle between Marshal Tito's communist Chetniks and the government Partisan forces under Colonel Mihailovic, she and her family spent seven years in a refugee camp at Bologna. Eventually her brother migrated to Australia and was able to sponsor Angela and their two sisters to follow him to the Snowy Mountains, where work was available because of ongoing development of the giant hydro-electric scheme.

Somehow Angela slipped through the cracks in the medical checking system despite a health problem which she had developed as a child – tuberculosis of the spine. She obtained a job in Cooma as a wards-maid, but the heavy work soon took its toll on her back. She was sent to Canberra for major surgery and spent twelve months in hospital there learning to walk again. Unable to keep a job because of her small stature (four feet six inches – 370cms), lack of fluent English, and poor health, she had become severely depressed, and when I met her she was a patient in the psychiatric section of Canberra Hospital under the threat of being sent to a mental institution for life.

Angela happily settled in with us. She came to church and, amid a flood of tears, gave her life to Jesus, had prayer for healing of all her physical needs, and gave up smoking overnight. We were able to find work for her at the Reid Technical College, where she assisted the cooking teacher. She walked for fifteen minutes each way to and from the bus stop near the college, and stood all day scrubbing heavy pots and wiping benches, although her doctors had advised 'no standing' because of her major surgery. She was tired, but elated, that her back had given her no problems. Her subsequent six-monthly check ups at the hospital confirmed her feeling that she was completely healed.

Angela stayed with us for a year, and then moved to Melbourne, where she was able to find lighter work in a factory assembling biro pens. She was very happy to work in comfortable, clean surroundings doing something more suited to her small frame. She continued to live in Melbourne, later marrying a widower whom she met at her local church. Although her nerves, eventually diagnosed as bi-polar disorder, have given her an occasional rough passage over the years, her tuberculosis has never returned and her strong Christian faith remains.

ROBYN

In 1970, when I thought I had finished collecting children, we experienced a major surprise and upheaval in our lives. I had returned to part-time secretarial work at CSIRO (Commonwealth Scientific and Industrial Research Organization) as the children were all at school. The laboratories were five minutes walk away, or one minute's drive, at the end of our street.

One very wet day I was driving home when, in a collision with another car, I was thrown from the vehicle and, according to witnesses, hit my head on a street light pole when I landed on the nature strip. I regained consciousness in the ambulance, and heard myself speaking in the prayer language I had received at the time of my water baptism, and repeating the name and phone number of the pastor of the church we were attending. After several hours in hospital undergoing tests I was allowed to go home, with strict instructions not to go to sleep too soon in case I lapsed into unconsciousness. Miraculously, apart from a headache and a few bruises, no further damage was detected.

Imagine the excitement when a few weeks later it became apparent that, at the age of forty two, I was pregnant. Helen, by then an outspoken young lady of nine years, summed it up: "Oh well, when Sarah was ninety nine God put new life into her, and she had a baby." To my knowledge though, he didn't use a car accident to achieve that result! Miracles come in many ways.

Robyn was six weeks premature, a little jaundiced, but a full seven and a half pounds in weight. She was pretty, alert and lovable, but she cried a lot. After a year of uncertainty we discovered she was profoundly deaf. And then we cried.

We explored many avenues to help her hear and speak, but to no avail. Against advice we bought a signing dictionary from Victoria because she was starting to use her own signs to communicate, and we began to sign to her at home. We were criticized by the oralist authorities in Canberra who said we must concentrate on trying to get her to speak, but at least it was no longer like living with a child shut away from us in a sound-proof glass cage. We encouraged her to read. We labelled everything in the house and took to carrying notepaper and pens to write down the names of things outdoors.

Our decision was later validated by Robyn's progress through the school system, ahead of her peers, as well as her understanding and fluency in written language. Socially however, life at school was often difficult for Robyn. There were times when I was heartbroken while I observed the rejection she suffered from children her own age.

Recently (in 2006) Robyn told me there has been an upsurge in hearing mothers of hearing children seeking enrolment in sign language classes. Research has established that using sign language with babies and children not yet able to communicate by speech enables them to talk to their mothers by signing, rather than just crying when they are hungry or uncomfortable.

NEW CHALLENGES

I have always been a great reader and fascinated by books. With a house full of children and books, it occurred to me that a second-hand bookshop conducted from home would be a great idea. I boldly named it 'Canberra Christian Book Exchange'. It proved popular, but after several months it became difficult to cope with people coming and going at odd hours of the day and night. At about this time Geoff left school and could not get work. I decided to expand the idea to a Christian bookshop/coffee shop in the city, calling it 'Agape Oasis', selling both new and second-hand Christian books. Geoff was employed to help me run it. After a couple of years he obtained a position at the Government Printing Office as a proofreader, so we closed the business. It had been a lot of fun, but a financial disaster. My accountant said it should have been registered as a philanthropic society as I have a tendency to give things away if I think someone needs them. My few business enterprises have not been very profitable!

An unforeseen change of career was just around the corner. For some years after coming into the new and close relationship with God I was active in Christian-based women's organisations and prayer fellowships. I also produced a small monthly newsletter, which grew out of my concern for social justice issues, and a perceived need to alert church folk to damaging trends that were threatening the fabric of our lives and families. I wrote many letters to newspapers along similar lines, believing that God had given me a new depth of understanding that I should voice in any way possible.

These activities brought my name to the notice of the Australian Family Association, who approached me to stand for election as number two on their Family Team ticket for the ACT House of Assembly in 1982. To our great surprise I was elected Family Team Member for Fraser. Suddenly I was plunged into an unfamiliar lifestyle. I felt like Alice in Wonderland much of the time. With my Family Team colleague, Mrs Bev Cains, I was allotted an office in the Council Chambers. People would call in or ring me there, or at home, with the most diverse problems, always expecting prompt solutions.

I believe God gave me this opportunity to be a voice, along with others, for righteousness in the nation. Events and comments made over the years have affirmed my belief. When the House of Assembly was disbanded in 1986, in preparation for ACT self government, a journalist assured me my presence there had definitely changed the atmosphere in the House. Just recently, nearly twenty years later, I received a card from a former colleague conveying a similar message. We can be encouraged, I think, that although we may be unaware of it at the time, nothing we do in God's strength goes to waste.

JIM

Meanwhile, Jim patiently supported me, dug in the vegetable garden and built fences and sheds to keep in the goats we had for milk, and the chickens we kept for eggs, on our quarter-acre suburban block. He walked or rode his bicycle to the office each day so that I could have the car. He held a Senior Research Officer position in a government department and was consistently involved in regional planning and hydrological developments such as the Snowy Mountains Scheme.

Jim was normally a quiet and reserved man. He found it difficult to openly express affection or to discuss emotional issues, as did many men in our generation. I once complained about this to a male colleague at work. His reply, which I still vividly recall, was, "Some men express love by giving their wives a car to drive around in" - which was exactly my situation at the time.

There were occasions though, when, for reasons that were not always apparent, Jim would explode in outbursts of anger of the type we often see exhibited in road rage today. This made life for the rest of us rather like living in the vicinity of an active volcano, and the safest defense similar to escaping from a lava flow – disappear until it cooled down!

I do not pretend to understand fully even now the reason for such eruptions. Sometimes there were apparent triggers, like the time the pet goat ring-barked the apple tree. Other times there were no causes we were aware of. Possible explanations could be that traumas he suffered through the death of his father from an unexplained suicide when he was just seven years old, and his own war service, contributed to an undiagnosed stress disorder. This might also have been responsible for his high blood pressure, not recognized until many years later. In any event, our marriage survived fifty-five years, until Jim's death in 2002.

For me, a remark Jim made at his 90th birthday celebration, is something precious which I can use to balance out any negatives. In a voice fading with the onset of his last years, he said: "When I visited a fortune teller in my younger days, she told me I would marry a wonderful woman, and I did." In the following months, with my failing hearing and his fading voice, we had even greater difficulties in the area of communication. Although I had waited a long time to hear those encouraging words, I am so glad I eventually did.

Jim regularly took all of us who were family at the time on caravan holidays. At some stage we invariably finished up near a large dam. Being a hydrology engineer he just loved dams! I cannot remember him ever being sick through those hectic years. When, in his early eighties, he had a cataract removed from his left eye, he was asked by the nursing sister for details of any previous surgery. After thinking for a while he said quite seriously, "I once had a large splinter removed from my thumb!"

FIGHTING INJUSTICE

In 1982, a lady who later became a very dear friend, Ros Nolan, rang and asked me as a member of the Advisory Council to, "Please do something about Lindy Chamberlain," whom she believed had been wrongfully convicted of killing her baby daughter. Although it was somewhat outside the realm of local politics, I tried to please all my constituents, and so I began investigating the matter. I rang Lindy's solicitor who said it was the worst case of justice gone wrong that he had ever seen. The local Adventist pastor, who knew the Chamberlains personally, told me that neither of them could ever be guilty of such a crime. When I rang the witnesses who were at the campground at Ayers Rock on the night the baby disappeared they, too, said they were convinced that something had malfunctioned in our justice system.

As a family we became very involved in the Chamberlain case. I wrote to Lindy in prison, kept in touch with her legal team and regularly sent out newsletters to try to correct some of the misinformation that the major newspapers were presenting as fact. All this action took place in a large caravan in our back garden with a typewriter, a photocopier and the help of a team of volunteers.

Well known Australian sculptor, Guy Boyd, in Melbourne, also took up the cause to fight for justice on Lindy's behalf. He and I were the co-ordinators for the 136,000 petitions that were gathered from all over

Australia and overseas, and presented to the Governor General in Canberra asking for a review of the case and the freeing of Lindy from Darwin prison. I was privileged to be visiting Ayers Rock with Jim and Robyn and her friend Sally on the day that the Chamberlains were finally exonerated by a Darwin court in 1987.

Because of the publicity around all our activities with the Lindy Chamberlain case we began to receive requests for help from other prisoners and their families who believed they were also victims of injustice. I really could not justify continuing to campaign on such a large scale under the auspices of the ACT Advisory Council, so I set up a separate non-profit, non-party political, non-denominational organisation with a band of professional men and women to assist, and titled it the National Freedom Council. Our aim was to promote belief in God and educate the nation in functioning according to Christian principles and to fight for victims of injustice. We gave assistance to as many as we could over a period of years.

MOVE TO QUEENSLAND

One by one the children left home. Robyn, being so much younger than the others, was still with us. In 1987, with Jim now retired from work and busily engaged in writing his family history, we decided to move to Brisbane so Robyn could be trained at Griffith University as a Teacher of the deaf, an opportunity that was not available in Canberra. In Brisbane she was able to participate in the worship and life of the Garden City

Church, Mt Gravatt, where there was a large congregation of deaf young people. Her social life changed dramatically and she met her future husband Simon there. Simon is also hearing impaired.

I continued to work with the National Freedom Council, endeavouring to assist a number of prisoners who claimed they had been wrongfully convicted, but it was difficult to function in Queensland without the network of support I had in Canberra.

In 1989, while recovering from the excitement of Expo and forty two house guests during the previous year, I was still working on a long-standing case of injustice about which I was writing a book. I undertook a fifteen week Private Investigator Course, which I thought might improve my investigative skills. We had some very interesting and humorous moments in our sleuthing training, including several surveillance operations, and I managed to pass the course. I was rather taken aback when I was offered a job with the company who had trained us. I declined – with thanks! It was one thing to do the training, and quite another to contemplate serious sleuthing on a full-time basis.

****

By 1994, with all the children flown the nest, I felt that my priority should now be to spend quality time with my husband, this man who had so generously shared me with others over many years. We moved into a Lutheran Retirement complex near Burleigh Heads on the Gold Coast, where Jim found fulfilment in the various activities available and built friendships with other residents. During this time I attended a monthly meeting of Gold Coast Writers as well as a small poet's forum on alternate Saturday afternoons, and won several prizes in performance poetry competitions. I took up quilting and spent most evenings hand piecing quilts in order to keep Jim company while he was watching television. I tried to give his requirements first place until his passing in March 2002, at the age of ninety-one years.

I had been unable to find a publisher for my major work, a detailed study of the Kim Barry murder case, but was more successful with a self-published collection of my poetry in early 2002. A poetry-diary was also published in England in 2003.

Alone after a marriage that lasted almost fifty six years, I moved across the Queensland border to Tweed Heads, to a cottage in an over fifties complex on the Cobaki Broadwater in West Tweed Heads. The northern rivers area of New South Wales is a wonderland of beaches, rivers, lakes and mountains. Its natural beauty has so far largely escaped the high rise concrete jungle spreading south from Surfers Paradise on the Gold Coast.

With lowered energy levels due to a persistent physical problem, my main priorities were to spend time with family and friends and the occasional person in need of a helping hand, along with daily fellowship with my Lord in prayer and in study of his Word. In

2005 I was diagnosed with severe sleep apnoea and was fitted with a night breathing CPAP machine. This improved my health considerably.

In January 2006 I moved back to Brisbane to be closer to Helen, Robyn and Geoff. The hustle and bustle of the city replaced the bucolic charm of the Tweed Valley, but I can travel back there to visit at any time. A computer, printer/copier, keyboard, CD player, telephone and TV vie for space in my small unit, but its size means less housework and more time to enjoy the contacts these conveniences allow.

Living by choice among older people on modest incomes, I am very aware of the difficulties and disappointments they face in a throw-away culture, where old is neglected or discarded in favour of new. Abuse of the elderly takes many forms, and has given me a new cause to address.

My family is now scattered around Australia. Lesley worked in Canberra after leaving school, then moved to South Australia to study at Adelaide Teacher's College, eventually marrying and settling in Adelaide. Her two children are now both parents themselves, and Lesley enjoys her role of grandmother, as well as voluntary work with environmental groups and travelling with husband Hans.

Claire continues to live in Canberra, where she studied and worked for many years at the Australian National University in the disciplines of sociology and political studies, achieving a Ph.D. in sociology in 2002. Her two sons are independent and busy working in their own fields, leaving opportunities for Claire and husband Leigh to travel interstate with work commitments as well as enjoying overseas holidays.

Helen grew into a young lady with a passion for horses, cooking, craft, and four-wheel driving. She lives in Brisbane, where she spent some hard years raising her two children alone after her husband moved overseas permanently. She is currently studying an Events Management course, and is engaged to be married to David, whom we are all happy to welcome into the family. Helen was reunited with her birth mother in Queensland around 1996. This lady, also named Betty, has told me she is very grateful Helen was raised with our family. She was not in a position to take care of a baby when Helen was born, but has enjoyed getting to know her over recent years. For all of us this has been a positive experience.

Geoff lives within a half-hour drive of my present home in Brisbane and I see him frequently. He has been a great support to me since Jim's death. He works with a Christian lighting and sound company. Up to this time Geoff has felt no need to trace his birth family, although he knows enough of his background to make that possible.

In 1991 Robyn graduated with a Bachelor of Teaching from Griffith University. It was a proud day for all of us. Her own experiences convinced her that hearing impaired children benefit greatly from instruction by teachers who can fully identify with their needs. She taught deaf children in Hobart, Tasmania, for twelve years, where she lived with her husband and children until returning to Brisbane in 2006. She was the first deaf teacher of the deaf in Tasmania.

REFLECTIONS

Looking back through our lives I suppose we all see things we would do differently if we could change the course of events. At sixty I thought I had perhaps by then gained enough experience and maturity to make a much better job of marriage and raising a family than I did at eighteen. Nearer eighty, I now believe our difficulties and mistakes are all part of the process required to mould us into shape for our eternal destiny. Sometimes we perceive words and actions as we interpret them, rather than as they possibly are, or are intended to be. People who hurt us have often been themselves emotionally damaged by events in their own past. One day we may discover that some of the things we found hard to handle were so because we misunderstood. Like many others, I gained much from the Biblical tale of Job, and stories of modern day men and women who have continued to love God and their fellows in circumstances far more difficult than anything I ever had to face.

I am surprised when someone tells me my words, actions or example helped them through their own rough spots, though I am aware that God uses us in unrecognised ways as we stay tuned in to him (II Corinthians 1:4). The beautiful Prayer of St Francis - "Lord make me a channel of your peace ..." has meant a lot to me ever since I came across it many years ago. Perhaps God has answered that prayer for me.

Corrie Ten Boom, the Dutch lady who suffered so much in the concentration camps at the hands of Hitler's henchmen, and lived to bless millions with her books and lectures, described life as a woven fabric, of which we see only the underside. We puzzle over dark threads and apparently meaningless mixtures of shapes and colours. God, however, sees it from the other side, a beautiful completed work of His weaving. One day, we shall see it too and will understand the weaving of the fabric of our life.

The night I first experienced the closeness of God's presence and spoke in the prayer language I had never learned, I was sure I heard Jesus say in my heart, "Put your hand in my hand Betty, and follow me". To me, Christianity is as simple as that.

Unlike the little brown duck in the poem that appeared to belong to no-one, I have come to know I am loved by God and belong to Him. He has taught me to trust.

Life's tapestry consists of threads
of joy and sorrow, laughter and tears,
good days and bad.

If we could see beyond the veil
of our earthly existence,
we would perhaps find it easier
to handle the difficult times.

No matter how dark the clouds
or how destructive the storm,
the wind will abate and
the sun shine again.

Betty Hocking

Betty and Jim on their wedding day, July 1946.

Betty just home from hospital with baby Robyn, Jim and
the children.

Betty (fourth from left) with all her natural siblings for the first time, January 1960.

Betty (second from left) with members of the Family Team at the launch of their 1982 ACT election campaign. Picture 'Courtesy ACT Heritage Library, *The Canberra Times* Collection'.

Angela

Betty with Lindy Chamberlain at the launch of Lindy's
book 'Through my eyes',   October 1990.

Betty and Jim at a family wedding in Adelaide, 1994.

Jim's 90th birthday, 2000. Left to right: Helen, Betty, Jim, Lesley, Geoff, and Claire, Robyn in Tasmania at the time.

JENNY ROBERTSON

When I first met Jenny she impressed me as a serene, quietly spoken, gracious woman, who constantly strives for excellence in weaving, her vocation in life. This impression has deepened as the years have gone by. She is innovative, skilful and artistic; a forward thinker.

Jenny tells of her struggle to adjust to the many changes in her life when she migrated to Australia from the UK as a young bride, pregnant with her first child, and how she came to a place of acceptance and peace. Part of this healing process included her miraculous healing from Chron's disease.

Coming from the lush green countryside of the UK, Jenny grew to love the stark beauty of the Australian landscape and has incorporated its striking natural elements into her weaving, creating products that are uniquely Australian.

A quiet achiever and a visionary, she is committed to using and developing her abilities to glorify God and bringing blessing to others.

Woven Threads

JENNY'S STORY

I stood in the Australian outback surrounded by the vivid contrasts of the blazing white salt lake, the soft grey-green of the saltbush, the brilliant red sand dunes, the pink and orange succulents surviving the heat and dryness around them, and my heart began to change towards this harsh country to which I had migrated with my new husband. We camped in the Australian bush for a week, and my longing for the lush green English countryside began to fade as I saw and absorbed a different beauty all around me. I became excited about the idea of translating this beauty into cloth that I would weave using the finest Australian merino wool.

That moment was an intimate experience that touched my spirit. I began to appreciate God's creation on the other side of the world in quite a different way. I felt a change within me as I embraced life in this new country. From that time on, my work with textiles and weaving evolved out of my personal experience with the unique Australian flora and landscape.

EARLY THREADS OF LIFE

I grew up in a small village in Somerset, in the United Kingdom. My love for creating beautiful garments began at an early age while watching my mother sew. She was a dressmaker and a tailoress, and my sister and I loved to watch her. When we were quite young she taught us to hand sew our doll's clothes, then, when we were old enough, we were allowed to use the electric sewing machine and progressed to making our own dresses.

After completing Primary School, I went to Worle Secondary School, Somerset, and was blessed with an excellent art teacher. I found great pleasure and satisfaction in studying art and painting. I also attended sewing classes, but I found them extremely boring since I had completed much more complicated sewing projects at home with my mother.

My sister and I often visited our grandparents during the long summer holidays. On one vacation we visited my mother's brother. This was a fascinating experience for me, because it was my first encounter with the artistic world. My uncle was an artist who lived in a tiny bed-sitter in Marlow beside the beautiful Thames River. Easels were scattered throughout his flat, with oil paints oozing everywhere. His bed was tucked away in the corner and I can remember thinking, "Wow, you can really live like this!" I had never seen anything like it. His art work inspired me. This was the first time I had seen someone working professionally as an artist and thoroughly enjoying his work and lifestyle. He also taught painting at Buckinghamshire College of Higher Education. This gave me hope that perhaps one day I could do something similar.

I was very keen to pursue a career in the Arts but my father was not happy about it because he felt that I would not be able to earn a living. In his opinion such a career carried the stigma associated with the bohemian lifestyle of many artists. My mother, on the other hand, was more supportive because her brother was a successful painter.

I acquired my first taste of working with textiles in a course involving experiments with printing techniques on fabric. This was part of a foundation Arts Course at the local Technical College, which I completed while studying for my 'A' Levels (Year 12 equivalent). Although I had no knowledge of looms or how to prepare them, I became interested in the whole concept of weaving. I borrowed some books from the library and made a cardboard sharp-edged board, around which I could wind threads that I had dyed with ink. I then tried to weave threads through and across, experimenting with the most primitive form of weaving - plain weave on cardboard. Although I didn't fully understand the process, I was intrigued by the interlacing of threads and the pattern structure they formed.

After I finished the Arts Course I took a year off and worked for an architectural practice in Bristol while I considered my future career choices. Although I loved art and painting, I could see that the field of textiles, which I also loved, had more potential for the foundation of a vocation. I visited some Colleges around the country who offered textile degree courses. A friend of mine was studying at West Surrey College of Art and Design in Farnham, Surrey, about an hour's train journey from London. This was a college with extremely high standards that demanded a lot of their students, had fantastic resources and teachers, and produced top quality work. The college consistently got students accepted into the Royal College of Art, which was only open to the top echelon of students, for their Master's study programme. West Surrey's main focus was incorporating both the artistic and technical aspects of the creative process to produce innovative textiles. This appealed to me, as the course was well balanced and made a strong base to work from.

Although it was very competitive for placements, I went for an interview and was delighted to be accepted to study at the college in Farnham. I could see that the course would provide me with the skills needed to establish my own professional studio, which was my vision for the future. The learning process would give me a vehicle for expressing the ideas in my heart as well as an opportunity to use my artistic gifts and to develop my business acumen.

During the first year of the course in Farnham the students were introduced to weaving. We commenced with the very first step - the raw materials. We prepared the fleece, combed and carded it, spun and plied our own yarn. Then we made warps, and learnt how to set up a loom for the first time. I absolutely loved it. I knew this was what I wanted to do. It was such a rich and creative endeavour, and I enjoyed the whole process despite the fact that it took such a long time to set up. I loved the intricacy and the detail of woven textiles, studying individual threads and how they behaved, how they interlaced with one another to form a structure. By using different colours and textures I could create a whole dimension of patterns and designs, like oil painting on a canvas.

This was art in its most intricate form taking shape under my hands, and I was fascinated. My love from childhood for all things miniature and detailed could be expressed through weaving something beautiful. I could see endless possibilities and infinite combinations of different fibres, textures and colours — all coming together to form one unique garment or fabric. I was inspired!

STRANDS OF FAITH

From the age of about fourteen I had gradually slipped away from attending church and had started to question what Christianity was all about and what it meant in my life. I couldn't see how I could have a personal relationship with God, although I didn't doubt that God created the world and that he created us. I became friends with Sallyanne, a fellow student who was staying in the same apartment at the college hostel. There was something purposeful about her, although I couldn't put my finger on what it was. She was loving, generous, kind and considerate, a thoughtful person who was concerned about others. I gradually came to realise that she had a close relationship with God, and this was expressed through her life. We got on really well because we shared an interest in textiles and both loved to weave. We often visited each other's homes and I enjoyed attending church with her family.

When I was about halfway through the course, in 1983, the college planned an overseas trip to Italy as part of the students' industrial experience. My friend Sallyanne and I decided to go a little earlier, get a Eurail pass and extend our time in Europe to four weeks. By that time I had started reading a Bible that Sallyanne had given me for my birthday. We caught an overnight train from Paris to Venice and as Sallyanne hadn't been overseas before I gave her some helpful advice. "You must be careful with your belongings and make sure that you put all your valuable things underneath the pillow if you want to go to sleep." However, I didn't take my own advice and must have fallen asleep, only to wake up and find my wallet missing and all my money gone. I was devastated that this had happened right at the beginning of our trip.

When we arrived in Venice I didn't really know what I was going to do. Sallyanne was worried, but she said that I needed to trust God to show me why this had happened. As I read my Bible I said to God, "I do trust you, and I am trying not to feel that I am being punished in any way, but can you please show me where you are in this?" A little later on I checked right through my bag to make sure nothing else was missing. Fortunately nothing else had been taken.

We looked everywhere for accommodation, and eventually stayed for a couple of blissfully quiet and peaceful nights in a convent on an island before we travelled down to Ravenna to the Youth Hostel. When we arrived in Ravenna I began to unpack my bag - and to my utter amazement I found a number of crisp new Italian currency notes in there. I had absolutely no idea where they had come from. When I took them out they smelt of printer's ink and they were sparkling and new. Sallyanne burst into tears and thanked God for this answer to her prayers!

This miracle just about made up all the money I had lost. I knew that God had met with me. It was such a real and personal experience of God's provision for me that I was deeply moved. That evening I gave my life to Him. After the commitment I had made to God I was overwhelmed by the vivid and dramatic portrayal of many Bible stories in the early Byzantine Ravenna mosaics we saw in the churches. The incredible colours of the mosaics and the way they were presented inspired me.

It seemed as if God had lit up my life and I could see things more clearly. I became increasingly aware of the world and people around me. Those first few days were so uplifting. This was the beginning of my walk with God. It was as if He challenged me to trust Him to provide for me, and this challenge has continued throughout my life. I have faced many situations where I have just had to trust God for the answers.

When the trip finished and we returned to the college in Surrey I started to attend the Baptist Church with Sallyanne, along with a number of other students. Participation in that fellowship was like being caught up in a revival - there was such enthusiasm and excitement amongst the students. A few months later I was baptized in water. On the evening of my baptism I told the congregation what God had done, and how I had come to believe in Him. I wasn't prepared for the mixed reactions that I had from people in the church because they found my story quite confronting. God's provision for me during our overseas trip was a physical, visible, tangible miracle, and not everyone could accept it.

Before I finished my studies at West Surrey I applied to the Royal College of Art in London to do my Master's studies. The application process to attend this college was highly competitive and involved submitting a portfolio of artwork and textiles. Only a few were then chosen to attend for an interview. Out of all the applicants only six from the whole of the UK were chosen for each specialisation. I was delighted to hear that I had been accepted. The fees were very high, but God had shown me quite clearly from the scriptures that I should go there, even though I had no financial means to pay. I had read a verse in the Old Testament where God promised milk and honey without expense and I felt that He was challenging me to trust him to provide for me if I would take the step of faith to go.

I went to see the Bursar just after I arrived and, although I was extremely nervous as I sat in his office, I shared with him the promise that God had given me that He would provide for me. To my great relief I was given a bursary which covered my fees as well as a living allowance. This was a wonderful provision of God.

I started to look for work. I was prepared to take anything that was available in local supermarkets or stores but was fortunate to obtain an interesting job at the Design Centre in Haymarket. The Centre held exhibitions as well as running a café, gallery and retail area for books and art objects. The left-over sandwiches and pastries from the café that I took back to our student accommodation after work were a treat greatly appreciated by my fellow students!

MEETING CHRIS

I met Chris, an Australian student studying for a Master's degree in Furniture Design, at the Royal College of Art in September 1984, just a few days after I moved to London. Chris had been selected from over forty applicants from around the world and had gained the only overseas place available. He had travelled to the UK from Perth, Western Australia, where his family lived.

After leaving school Chris had completed an apprenticeship, gaining carpentry and joinery qualifications. He had used these skills in a Government cultural development scheme which involved him travelling to remote areas of Western Australia teaching Aboriginal communities how to build cyclone proof housing. He did this for seven years and then decided to attend Curtin University to undertake further studies. He started a degree in education and then switched to the Art Department, where he studied Three Dimensional Design in Wood. It was following these university studies that he was awarded the scholarship to study in the UK for his Master's qualifications.

We both lived at the student accommodation in South Kensington, London, and shared common interests in furniture and textiles. When I met Chris my heart went out to him. He was shy and quite withdrawn, and was finding it difficult to adjust to living in a new country.

At this time I was attending a home fellowship group led by an Australian and we began to pray for Chris. Chris and I started to spend time together and had some discussions and arguments about the Bible and what it meant. I felt that God gave me answers to Chris's questions. I could tell that Chris was seeking for truth. One day he asked if he could come to church with me, and the words of the speaker that evening really touched his heart. From then on God continued to show Chris that He was there for him personally. A few months later, just after Christmas, we were at my parent's house. It was very cold, but Chris decided to go for a walk by himself in the woods opposite the house. When he came back he said, "I have come home." I knew exactly what he meant. His whole countenance had changed and he had become very peaceful. As we spent more time together our relationship deepened, and it became clear that we would get married.

Although my relationship with Chris was going well, my art studies fared less well. When I commenced my studies at the Royal College of Art there had been a change in the Head of Department and the new Head wasn't supportive of the work of a number of the weaving students. He had limited perception and experience of how things should be done in textile design. This made it difficult for me because the industrial projects we were asked to complete as part of our studies were not in line with my Master's proposal. This became more and more frustrating as time went on and I could not freely develop my ideas and my project.

I eventually left the Royal College of Art after the fourth term, before my course finished, and returned to Farnham to finish off the textile work that I had started for my Masters. This meant that I gave up my Master's qualification, but I wasn't concerned so much about the qualification as I was about the experience and skills that I could gain and continue to develop.

This was in February 1986 and our wedding date had been set for August. Chris and I spoke on the phone often during the week and saw each other on weekends. We had some supportive Christian friends and often prayed together, which was particularly uplifting during the low ebb I experienced after leaving the college. On one occasion, while we were praying, I sensed a strong presence of the Lord. I cried out to him to use me. I was willing to give up weaving at that point. Some pertinent words of encouragement given at the time suggested that God would raise me up as a light in the world through my weaving, and that I would be brought before royalty. This seemed an impossibility to me because I couldn't see how it could ever come to pass, but I knew that God was able to do the impossible if I just trusted in Him and followed my vision. So I continued my weaving with a renewed enthusiasm and a sense of God's calling on my life.

The upholstered furniture that Chris and I managed to complete by May/June of that year was innovative and received a lot of publicity. The furniture was designed to interact with the human form in a unique way, and gave consideration to both ergonomic and aesthetic concerns. It attracted international attention, and Vico Magistretti, a famous Italian architect and visiting lecturer at the Royal College, was excited by our designs. He recommended us to Cassina, an international furniture design company, who then invited us to go to Italy and work with their company. Since we were about to be married we postponed the trip until after our wedding.

Chris and I were married on the 9th August 1986, on a beautiful sunny day in the same Anglican Church in Somerset where my parents had been married, which made it very special for us. My brother catered for the wedding reception, held in a beautiful old English garden, a brave, or foolish, decision considering the English climate, especially as it poured with rain the day before and the day after the wedding. It was exciting to begin our life together, exploring and developing the creative gifts given to us by God, and discovering His plan for our lives.

A month later we accepted the invitation to work with Cassina at their headquarters in a tiny village just north of Milan in Italy, where we were their guests for nearly four weeks. We stayed in a five star villa set in lovely surroundings, at their expense, with pocket money and a red Renault provided for us to drive. We felt as if we had entered another world. Chris worked with the designers in the factory during the week, while I spent time with the Director's wife, who was in charge of the textiles. I assisted her with some colour consultancy, which involved forecasting colour groups of textiles for future production of upholstered furniture. We also made trips to textile industries on the edge of Lake Como. On the weekends Chris and I drove the Renault around the local area and explored the beautiful Italian countryside. We had a fantastic time and regarded it as our honeymoon.

MOVE TO AUSTRALIA

When we returned to the UK a month later we decided to cover our options by applying for me to migrate to Australia, and also for Chris to extend his stay in the UK because his student visa had expired. However, we were told that Chris could not stay in the UK so we made preparations to migrate to Australia.

The direct flights were all booked out, so we had

to fly with a Russian airline via Moscow, India, and Kuala Lumpur to get to Australia. We had to organise the flights before I knew whether my application to migrate had been approved. When we went to visit my parents in Somerset to say goodbye, we found that the letter from the Australian Embassy advising that my application to migrate was approved, had arrived there earlier that same day. If this had not come through we would have lost all the money we had paid for our fares. This would have been disastrous because we had just finished studying, we had no financial resources behind us, and we had borrowed the money. Later we discovered the fares were actually part of a wedding gift, but we would still have lost the money if we had to cancel our flights. We were given some words of encouragement from a friend the day before we left, urging us to trust God and continue to look to Him. We didn't fully understand the importance of this at the time, but as events unfolded we realised the significance of those words.

On our departure day in December 1986, when we were ready to leave for Heathrow Airport, Chris suddenly realised that he had lost his passport and couldn't find it anywhere, despite a frantic search. When we checked in without Chris's passport the Russian airline questioned Chris closely, while I fervently prayed. Miraculously, they allowed us to board without it. This was an amazing display of God's provision for us. An additional blessing was our upgrade to first class seats because we were the last ones to board the plane. We enjoyed a luxury trip complete with some expensive Lindt chocolates given to us by a friend as we were leaving!

We had heard stories about people being sent back to the UK from Moscow because they didn't have a return ticket so we were very apprehensive about travelling without Chris's passport. In Moscow we were stopped by Passport Control and questioned and searched, but we were allowed to continue on through Delhi, India, without any problems. When we arrived at Kuala Lumpur, where we were due to stay for two days, the airport authorities were going to send us on to Sydney on the next flight. Since our destination was Perth, and we had no money for extra air fares, we told them that this would cause major problems for us. To our relief, the Malaysian authorities changed their minds and decided instead to put us under house arrest, and accommodated us in the airport hotel.

The next day, at the Australian Embassy, I received my first experience of the laid back Australian 'no worries' attitude and culture. One of the officers gave Chris an identity document with stamps all over it, which the Malaysian authorities accepted, and so we were able to explore and see the sights in Kuala Lumpur. When we left the country the staff from the airport authorities came and got our bags for us and gave us a discount on our account at the hotel. What a turn-around this was from our initial reception!

We arrived in Perth, Western Australia, early on the morning of Chris's mother's birthday, which delighted her. I was a few months pregnant with our first child and felt that we were a bit like Mary and Joseph, travelling so far just before Christmas. After we had settled in and spent some time getting to know his family, Chris started to look for a job. We were excited because we believed God had brought us this far and that He was going to show us what He wanted us to do straight away. We had expectations of how we thought He would work – but He didn't meet any of these. Here we were, newly married, just arrived in Australia from the middle of winter to the middle of summer, me pregnant, trying to find somewhere to live and looking for work, all of which proved to be difficult and stressful.

Having stayed with Chris's parents for five months we decided to move out after Ben's birth. We moved into a lovely little cottage in Fremantle the day I came out of hospital with Ben. Although we were only there for a short time I have fond memories of that house.

Chris acquired a temporary job for a few months helping to curate a collection of artworks at Curtin University. We did not have a car so he had to leave at seven a.m. to catch two buses to get to work, and often didn't get home until seven p.m. This was hard at first because I didn't know anyone in Fremantle. Eventually we found a church to attend and started to make some friends.

During this time, while we were considering a more permanent home, I felt that God was saying to me, "What would you like in a home?" I felt that He wanted me to be quite specific, so we started to build up a list of all our desires and dreams for a house. Our dream house would be near the sea, have black and white tiles on the kitchen floor, have fruit trees in the garden, be within walking distance from the town and the shops, and have plain painted walls, wooden floors and a pot belly stove. Little did we know that all these desires for our dream home were part of the renovations being completed by a young couple in our church.

We met this couple at the church one day, not long after they had finished their renovations, and they told us that they had been offered a position on Rottnest Island, just off the WA coast near Fremantle, which is where they had always wanted to live. We did not know at the time that they were looking and praying for a family from the church to rent their house. One Sunday they invited us to their home for coffee after the church service. While we were there, it suddenly dawned on Chris that this house had everything we had asked for in our dream home. On our way home we became very excited and decided to enquire if it was available for rent. We were thrilled to find that it was, the rent was hardly any more expensive than where we were living, and the couple were happy to rent it to us. We had ten wonderful years in that house and were thankful for the generosity and abundant provision of God.

Late in 1987 Chris was awarded a business set up grant from the Crafts Council in Australia, which covered about $10,000 worth of equipment. He established a large workshop space in an old hotel in

East Fremantle that was being leased out at artist studio rates from the local council, and purchased second hand equipment at cheap rates. He was then able to produce furniture and jewellery. Chris has broad skills with both wood and metals, and although he majored in furniture design for his Master's degree, his previous undergraduate degree had been a combination of furniture and jewellery.

FAMILY IN FREMANTLE

Our three sons were born in Fremantle. Ben was born in 1987, Tim in 1988, and David in 1991. I had three boys under the age of four for a few months, which was a busy time, but it meant that they grew up together and became really good friends. Part of our daily life was spent walking and swimming and enjoying the beach, something I had always loved having grown up by the seaside in the UK. We could walk into Fremantle. It was a lovely place to live.

Initially I had no loom and so I was unable to do any form of weaving. On one occasion, when visiting the Crafts Council in Perth, I saw a loom in the corridor of their building which wasn't being used. I made some enquiries and the Director and the Board of the Crafts Council were happy for me to take it and use it. It was a basic, little floor standing loom with four shafts and pedals on the floor that you could operate with your feet, but it worked really well. That was how I started weaving in Australia. It was quite a challenge for me to weave on such a simple loom. I had to re-think how

I worked and what I could do because the loom's functions were so basic compared to what I had trained on. To get satisfaction out of doing this was a completely different mind-set to working with a more complex loom. I started developing some new work, in the evenings mainly, and during the day sometimes when Chris's parents looked after one or two of the boys. With the work I did on this little loom I was able to exhibit occasionally and gradually build up my practice.

An interesting incident occurred in the earlier years we lived in Fremantle. We were now the proud possessors of a red and green Mini, which had been given to us by Chris's brother Noel. We had to park the Mini on the street because there were no driveways in our road. One day we became aware that someone was stealing petrol from our Mini and decided to change the petrol cap for a lockable one. As access to our petrol was no longer available the thief became angry and tipped the car on its side in the middle of the road! We received this news from the Ranger who knocked on our door early the next morning. Not long after this we changed the Mini for a van, and the same thing started to happen. Chris heard noises one night and when he went out to investigate, sure enough, there was a bucket and some pipe down by the van but the person had run off. In the process of stealing the petrol he had done quite a bit of damage to our van. I rang the police and eventually they caught the culprit.

By this time Chris and I had prayed about the whole situation and had forgiven the offender. He was told that if we wanted to take the thief to court we had to pay an amount up front to do this, for which we would not be reimbursed. The thief didn't think it was fair that we should have to pay, and so he decided of his own volition that he would come and pay us back for the damage he had caused to the van. Every week for at least ten weeks he knocked on the front door and handed us the money until he had paid off the amount in full. This was a most unexpected resolution to the situation, that demonstrated to us the power of prayer and forgiveness.

In 1988 Chris was given a commission to do some work for Elsje King, the Head of textiles at the University in Perth. She commissioned him to make her a desk and a chair, and through this we got to know her personally. She had just imported, at considerable expense, a little British loom that worked with a memory device. The late eighties were early days for computerised weaving, but she wasn't a weaver and didn't really know what to do with this loom. She hadn't set it up and offered it to me to use at no cost, although we did draw up a contract. It was one of few such looms within Australia. I am still not sure to this day why she actually bought and imported it. Perhaps it was God's provision for me because we did not have the means to buy anything like it.

At home in the studio room I started to weave on the new loom. It was quite small, like a table loom on a stand, with sixteen shafts, which potentially enabled me to weave complex patterns and two layers of cloth at least. But I had to be careful not to weave anything too heavy on it, which I found out by trial and error. It was such a blessing to have this loom, which was better than the ones I had trained on in the UK because it had a memory device. It enabled me to make designs that were not possible on a fully manual loom. This was another confirmation in my heart that I was in the right place in Australia, as it would have been impossible for me to have such a loom to work on in the UK.

HEALING TOUCH

After Tim's birth in October 1988, and over the next twelve months, I became chronically ill. Eventually I was admitted to hospital where they ran tests and discovered I had Crohn's disease. This can sometimes develop after giving birth. Dr Burrill Crohn named this disease in the late 1800's. It is an abnormal inflammation of the small bowel or colon which, in its most severe form can lead to removal of the intestines and being fed from a tube. It can also be fatal. I was put on a course of treatment for a week. During this time I had to leave Ben and Tim with Chris and his parents because I was just too ill to cope. When I came home I was still very ill, and received ongoing treatment for the next four to five months. However, through prayer I experienced God's healing power in a remarkable way. I believe the combination of the treatment, the rest, and God's healing touch all combined to cause the illness to recede to the point where I was completely healed, which is extremely rare. The doctors were amazed and I was so thankful to God for this answer to prayer.

The whole healing process was interesting because I felt that there were a lot of issues in my life that I had not dealt with. I had been through four major life changes in one year. I was married, I migrated to Australia, I gave birth to Ben, and we set up our own business – all in my first year of marriage. These are considered to be the most major changes that a person can make in a lifetime, and I had compressed them all into the space of twelve months. Added to this was the stress of having left my family knowing they were upset because I had left the 'mother country'. Apparently this is not uncommon for those who migrate to another country. Although on the surface I was happy with my new life in Australia, and deeply loved my husband and children and our beautiful home, I had suppressed a lot of the tension and anxiety involved in these changes. The illness forced me to deal with these issues.

When I was in hospital having many tests, one of the specialists came and sat down on my bed and asked me a perceptive question. He said, "Have you been carrying a heavy load?" His words were very discerning of my situation and made me aware that I needed to come to terms with all these changes and to arrive at a place of acceptance and peace. During the time I was confined to bed I went through a process of reflection and re-visiting my emotions and feelings, letting God into the places that were really hurting, and allowing Him to bring peace and healing to my soul.

By the time we went back to our home in Fremantle I felt I could truly call Australia my home and really mean it with all my heart.

Another experience that helped me during this period of adjustment occurred when our family went camping at Lake Baladjie, a salt lake in a nature reserve located in remote Western Australia, on the edge of the wheat belt and goldfields around Kalgoorlie. It was the most remarkable place in a remote area where you had to take all your own water and provisions. The children were quite young and we had a wonderful time cooking over an open fire and baking different bread every day in the wood fire, as well as enjoying delicious meals cooked in the camp oven.

This camping experience forced me to look at my surroundings with a fresh perspective, and I was able to appreciate the Australian landscape and vegetation in a way that I hadn't before. Previously I had longed for the lush English flora and had missed it so much. I now fell in love with Australian plants and their different colouring and textures. I began to think about creating work that expressed the idea of belonging, in relationship to the natural elements that I saw and experienced in Australia. I wanted to create work that was uniquely Australian, technically complex and aesthetically pleasing to look at. I also wanted to incorporate the emotional and the sensory elements through the creative process of using texture, structure, colour and fibre in woven textiles that would draw out a response from a broad range of people. I saw that I could use traditional European techniques of weaving but develop a new thematic visual language that was unique to Australia and to my personal experience. This was a very important time for my professional development.

Life was erratic in terms of an income since we didn't have any other form of support from the Government. It was a stressful time for us financially because we hardly had any money. In fact, for many years we were worse off than if we had been on Government benefits, which was a bit hard to accept. We had three small children to support and a lot of the time we were struggling to exist. It was often hard to see from one day to the next where the money would come from to pay the rent and put food on the table. Sometimes we would get money from winning art and craft awards and sometimes from a commission. Despite this, we were committed to developing our talents and abilities to the fullest extent possible as we strongly believed that they were gifts given to us by God and that we should use them to glorify Him.

From 1987 to 1991 we had a home fellowship group at our house and I always provided a cooked meal for them, although at times I didn't know where the food was going to come from. I have a vivid memory of one such time when I had nothing in my cupboard to prepare for dinner for the group. Just a couple of hours before the people were due to arrive our next door neighbour knocked on the door and said, "I have a bag of fish I thought you might be able to use" Naturally I was delighted to accept, and that night we all enjoyed a delicious meal of fish for dinner - a direct provision from God through my neighbour! Other times I came home to find grocery shopping on our doorstep, and one day even an anonymous present for me!

Late in 1990 Chris fell off a ladder in the workshop and broke his hip. This put him in bed for six weeks, in a lot of pain, and meant that he could not work. Fortunately I had earlier accepted an offer of some textile teaching at the university. During his illness Chris sat up in bed and drew in his sketch book. From his drawings he designed a knife set, which he entered in an international knife-making competition in Sakai, Japan. He won the grand prize. In February 1991 the Western Australian Government sent Chris to Japan for the award ceremony, which was a dream come true for him. The prize was a million yen, so our friends all joked that we were 'mill-yen-aires'. It was actually a reasonable amount of money. In the middle of this time, when we had very little money and were doing the best we could with what we had, God provided these trips or fundings as blessings into our lives. It was either poverty or riches – without much in between.

In 1992 I started to develop a range of woven double layered scarves produced with fine merino wool. This is a technique where two separate layers of cloth are woven simultaneously on the loom, intersecting to form designs on both sides. Two of the pieces from my early work were accepted into an

International Textile Competition in Japan, which was an incredible honour because the selection process was so rigorous. I was only the second Australian to get into this competition. I was able to apply for funding from the Australia Council, through the Commonwealth Government, to participate in the opening ceremony and they agreed to fund my trip. I was very excited because I had always wanted to go to Japan. I spent ten days in Kyoto and had the most interesting experiences absorbing the culture and looking at the artworks, textiles, buildings and gardens.

During 1993/94 I felt that God gave me a clear vision to work towards in my practice. I was still working on borrowed equipment, but I had a picture in my mind of working on a loom that was really flexible, on which I could develop and pursue my textile practice in the best possible way by semi-automating the production; having the loom wide enough to produce cloth up to 1.5 metres wide, which was a standard width for furnishings, but also to be able to weave in narrower widths, as well as different layered widths.

Chris and I decided that, because we had developed plans of various looms over the years, we would have sufficient knowledge and expertise, particularly Chris, to build a loom. In 1994 we put together another application to the Australia Council, the Commonwealth funding body. This was also successful. We purchased a large amount of Blackbutt wood and started to source other materials and pieces of equipment that we needed to build a loom. Some of the pieces Chris had to make out of special materials, and some we were able to buy pre-fabricated. It was a huge task, and it took three to four years part-time to finish.

I applied for funding again in 1997 to complete the computerisation part of the loom, because the initial funding was eaten up very quickly with the physical part of building the loom and purchasing the materials, even though we didn't take much out for labour. The computerisation grant was also approved, and enabled us to purchase the software. The writer of the programme in America was able to modify it for our needs to thirty two shafts, the maximum number you can have before it becomes a jacquard loom – which is a much more complex piece of equipment.

Many people do not realise that the jacquard loom developed in the early 1800's was actually the forerunner to the modern computer. It used a binary system of operation. Ironically, in the last ten years weaving software has been developed that works directly with a computer on a jacquard loom and you can now weave photographs if you want to. So technology has gone the full circle. A jacquard loom was far too expensive for us to purchase as the cost is about the same amount as buying a house. I felt that this was not justified for one person's use. However, I now had the next best thing, which gave me the capacity to work with multiple layers and complex weaving structures. This was a very exciting time.

MOVE TO CANBERRA

At the beginning of 1997 I was offered a part-time lecturing position with the Australian National University (ANU). We packed up everything in WA and moved our family to Canberra, originally thinking that it would be just for a year or so. While the move was a real blessing, it also had its trials and difficulties. It took a long time for the boys to adjust to living in Canberra as we had no extended family here. I continued to communicate with my family in the UK through phone calls, letters and photographs, but it was hard to enjoy close relationships from such a long distance.

At the end of my fixed term contract at the Uni we decided not to renew the lease on our rental house because we did not know whether my contract would be renewed. Like Abraham, who packed everything up and lived in tents for a time, we felt that this was what we should do. We packed all our goods, put them in storage, and headed out to the beautiful Cotter River to camp for the whole eight weeks of the summer holidays. The boys had a ball! We decided we would try to buy a cheap house that needed renovating, with a studio attached that we could use for our work. We had previously noticed an attractive house on the way to visit friends and when we discovered it was for sale we looked up the advertisement in the local paper, but considered it too expensive for our very limited budget.

Not long after we had moved into our temporary tent accommodation we were on our way into town when something went wrong with the van. We took it to the service station close to where we had previously lived, and waited for it to be fixed. While we were waiting I noticed that there was a real estate agent's office across the road and it happened to be the same one that was selling the house in which we were interested. I decided to go and make some enquiries. The agent tried to put us off at first. He said the house was almost sold and they were waiting for contracts to be exchanged. We found out that it was being sold for a lot less than the advertised selling price, so we went to have another look and decided it was the right house for us. We put in a bid and as the sale still hadn't been finalised our offer was accepted.

This home has been such a great blessing to our family, and it is now worth four to five times what we paid for it! It had a music studio that we adapted for our machinery, which was cheaper than renting a separate studio. Chris renovated and restored the house over a period of six or seven years while I was lecturing and weaving and earning the income for the family.

In September 1999 Chris and I exhibited our work at the Australian National Botanic Gardens Gallery during the Floriade festival. This was our first Canberra exhibition. I was weaving with black and white and then crossing over and working in colour, alternating between the two, which I really enjoy as they complement one another so well. One is full of contrast and is stark, and the other is full of nuances and subtleties. The end result is a rich design. Chris had received a grant to develop a series of teapots and vases in metal, working with native flora, specifically various species of eucalypts. We had an Ikebana florist, skilled in the particular art of Japanese floristry, who was able to interpret Chris's work and arrange the appropriate native flora in the vases for the exhibition. This exhibition attracted lots of people and created some wonderful openings.

NEW DOORS OF OPPORTUNITY

In the year 2000 I was given the most unexpected opportunity. Each professional member of Craft ACT had a colour image of their work published as a card with their details on the back. These cards then were put together to produce a book that was sent out to lots of different organisations and contacts around Australia. The ACT Chief Minister's Department selected me out of this book and wanted to purchase the piece of work that was displayed. I wondered why they wanted this particular piece so desperately. It was a red and gold offset double cloth scarf in fine merino wool featuring Gondwana fossilised plant images from early Australia – it was one of the earlier pieces I had made on my new loom. To my surprise, I found out that they wanted to give it to the Queen on her official visit to Canberra. The Chief Minister's Office phoned me on Friday before the Monday of the Queen's visit to ask me to present the scarf to Her Majesty. At the time I was out bush with the students at the Cotter River for the day and was unavailable. When I arrived home later in the day I was very surprised to receive the message that I was to meet the Queen. I didn't even have time to look for a new dress!

On the Monday morning I was at the Hotel Kurrajong preparing for the Queen's arrival. The Queen came into the patio area where we had set up a display stand with the scarf on it and I was the first person she met. We had a chat and I presented her with the scarf. She then moved on down the red carpet and met all the other dignitaries and local representatives. As she came back up the other side she met Chris and Ben, who had a special invitation to attend, and engaged in a chat to them.

We have a lovely collection of memories and photographs of this special meeting with the Queen, which went down well with the relatives in the UK. It brought back to my mind and heart the word that had been given to me some years ago that I would be brought before royalty. Although it had seemed impossible at the time, it had come to pass. God had opened another door of opportunity. I felt extremely honoured.

In September 2000 I visited Kyoto and Tokyo, Japan, as part of an ANU exchange programme. During the trip I visited the Nuno Corporation in Tokyo, who were keen to put my double cloth wraps into production in Japan. This company was considered to be at the forefront of contemporary textile production. The first production series came on the market in early 2001. This was a great encouragement and affirmation for me internationally.

A DOUBLE PORTION

At the beginning of 2001 I was asked by the Crafts Council of the ACT to hold an exhibition of my woven double cloths in their Gallery at its new location in Civic Square. I developed a series of offset double cloths where each layer overlapped, intersecting to form woven imagery. The exhibition was titled 'Double Portion', which had a twofold meaning for me. It reflected the generous and overflowing personal encouragement and blessing I had received from God over the years as well as relating to the technique I had developed with the double cloth weaving.

This exhibition featured in a television documentary made by the ABC for 'Snapshot', a state cultural programme. This was one of a number of documentaries of my work made by SBS and the ABC over the years. One was made for the ABC national television arts programme 'Coast to Coast' and featured the whole process of weaving, from how I sourced my initial inspiration and ideas, the field trips, drawings I made, how the computerisation process was incorporated, right through to the finished product.

AUSTRALIA COUNCIL FELLOWSHIP

Early in 2001 I wrote an application for an Australia Council Fellowship, a once in a lifetime grant to work on a special research project. This was an application for two years of funding to explore the thematic language between landscape, wool and the body, and to develop a series of triple cloth woven textiles. Triple cloth weaving is a most unusual form of weaving. Rare examples are seen internationally. It is highly complex, but it affords some interesting opportunities in terms of designing and making three dimensional fabric. You can achieve different patterns on each side, all of which relate to each other. I became quite fascinated by these techniques, particularly those made by the ancient Peruvian culture.

The application was successful. I was fortunate to be one of only three Australians to be awarded this visual arts and crafts Fellowship. It involved a number of field trips around the country, which we undertook as a family, travelling and camping, hiking, photographing, documenting and drawing, and then coming back to the studio and working from the information gathered.

On our first field trip in December 2001 we went to Tasmania for four weeks where we travelled, camped and hiked all around the National Parks and World Heritage areas. We spent time in the pristine wilderness of Cradle Mountain, hiked around some of the glacial lakes and over the mountains, gaining spectacular panoramic views despite the moody and inclement weather. Mt Field National Park was fascinating with seven different kinds of vegetation that we explored and photographed while we hiked through the lower rain forest areas right up into the exposed alpine terrain. On Christmas day we were barbecuing marinated turkey kebabs for lunch in the Central Lakes area when we were drenched by a dramatic rain storm and forced to run for cover. The following morning David caught a two kilogram trout in the lake, which we took to the tiny town of Ross, where we discovered an award winning bakery that offered bed and breakfast accommodation. We booked in for a night of respite from the wet weather, and enjoyed the most delightful wood-fired stuffed trout, wood-fired bread and delicious bakery cooked cakes that melted in our mouths, along with a warming log fire.

That trip was an awe inspiring time. We gathered lots of resources and books on flora that I could work from in the studio.

The next trip involved driving from Canberra to Western Australia, stopping off at all the National Parks along the way, and then driving back again. During the trip we spent time in the Flinders Ranges in South Australia, where I was intrigued by the effects of the light on the colours of the vegetation. The soft purple and green hues of the plants on the hillsides gently changed throughout the day to stunning sunsets reflected on the rock surfaces. We travelled 1,000 kilometres on the straight, flat road over the Nullarbor plains, where you can see a car coming from over fifty kilometres distance. The Fitzgerald River National Park was especially inspiring. This is an unusual Park, known for its vegetation that dates back to Gondwana, with many species of unusual and rare banksias, hakeas and eucalypts. It is one of the richest bio-diversity areas in the world. Driving into the park was like entering an ancient and different world.

This field trip was much more about the sense of a journey, and the way that you can create textiles that shift and change through the process of weaving. The metaphors became quite interesting, working between the primary experience of the field trips and telling the story by creating weaving that mirrored or echoed this.

The final field trip took six weeks. We drove 15,000 kilometres through the centre of Australia. We went hiking in the MacDonnell Ranges, through Ormiston Gorge, with its stunning scenery and reflected light. I walked ten kilometres around the base of Uluru and was impressed by its immense size as well as the interesting textured surfaces of the rock. The sunset at Uluru was magnificent with its changing colours from orange/brown to a luminous red then to a deep purple. We walked through the Valley of the Winds in the Olgas, and saw Kings Canyon and Stanley Chasm. Alice Springs was an interesting town, with lots of art galleries showing works of indigenous Central Australian artists, which we thoroughly enjoyed. We used Alice Springs as a base to explore the West MacDonnell Ranges.

We drove nearly 1,000 kilometres north in one day, which took us from the dry heat of Alice Springs to the hot and steamy weather of Elsey River. We paid a quick visit to the Mataranka Hot Springs along the way, and then travelled west to the Kimberleys in the top of Western Australia, staying at the Ord River. Late one afternoon I took a scenic flight that is considered to be one of the most spectacular flights in Australia. It covered from Kununurra to the Bungle Bungles in Purnululu National Park, flying over the Ord River and the Argyle Diamond Mine and Texas Downs Station. I took many photographs of the stunning scenery.

We spent some time in the Daly River area south of Darwin, where we first encountered crocodiles, from a reasonably safe distance, and the boys enjoyed barramundi fishing from a tinnie, a small aluminium boat. This was the first time we were able to visit an Aboriginal community without a permit, where they had developed an art gallery and centre that displayed examples of basketry, paintings and prints.

Our next stopover was in Darwin, where we spent a few days exploring and discovering its fascinating history. On a visit to a museum there we saw the stuffed body of 'Sweetie' an enormous fully grown crocodile (between eight to ten metres long) that had been known locally to be harmless, apart from an annoying habit of tipping people out of their boats. Unfortunately, the other crocodiles would then attack the hapless victims! When trying to move Sweetie to another location less popular with tourists he had died, so they decided to preserve his body and keep it in the museum.

We then travelled to Kakadu National Park for five days. This was a most unusual Park, very hot and steamy, with Aboriginal rock paintings, wetlands, lots of watery billabongs and beautiful birds. We took a cruise on one of the main water-ways, and saw crocodiles, water buffalo and lots of mangroves and unusual water plants.

On our journey home we retraced our steps to Alice Springs and visited the East MacDonnell ranges, before returning to Canberra. I eagerly anticipated coming back to the studio to work through what I had seen and experienced. I had accumulated many books and photos to supplement my resources and these have provided an ongoing source of inspiration for my weaving.

INTERNATIONAL OPPORTUNITIES

In 2003 I had another marvellous experience. I received funding from the ACT Government for a residency at the Fondazione Arte Della Seta in Florence, Italy, and for five weeks I was weaving silk velvet with different heights of pile called Cisele velvet. This was also three layered weaving, but it was working on very old equipment. Although it was time-consuming, manual work with extremely fine silk of about 2,000 threads per thirty centimetre of warp, so fine that I could hardly see the threads even with my glasses on, it was a fascinating experience to learn the process. I then began to research antique velvets and look at the historical stylistic periods of velvet, particularly in the renaissance time when they flowed through Europe and into France from Italy. This was an extraordinary period of history. I love to look at the European silk velvet, I find it very inspiring. Many vestments were made for the church, and today you can still view these exquisite materials in museum collections

In 2004 I held a solo exhibition to show the triple cloth work I had developed from the Australia Council Fellowship. This exhibition was held at Craft ACT, in Canberra, and a number of pieces were purchased for the collections of the National Gallery and the Art Gallery of South Australia. Other pieces were shown in exhibitions around the country. Following this, the majority of the triple cloths went to London, where I had my first solo exhibition. This was highly successful and all of the triple cloth wraps sold. It received a wonderful response from the public and from art critics. Triple cloth weaving is an unusual and complex form of weaving, akin to playing three dimensional chess.

During September 2004 I completed a residency in computerised jacquard weaving at the Centre for Contemporary Textiles in Montreal, Canada. This was a huge contrast from the old manual equipment I had used during the previous year in Italy. I was also able to attend an International Miniature Textile exhibition in Como, Italy, where some of my miniature textile pieces were exhibited.

A Fellowship from the ACT Government was granted to me in 2005 to develop a range of furnishing textiles based on historical woven structures, particularly French textiles from the sixteenth to the nineteenth century. At that time in history the weavers were located in the Lyons area in France and became renowned internationally for their weaving. Lyons was set up as a weaver's town, with secret underground passages called traboules, through which the silk was ferried when the weather was too bad to take it through the streets. It also provided security for transporting goods when needed. There were special houses built with four metre high ceilings to accommodate the height of the looms. The whole area has World Heritage listing and is a fascinating place to visit.

While I was there I visited the textile museum. This held an amazing collection of draw loom and jacquard textiles, with lots of samples of specially commissioned fabrics, such as those for Napolean and Josephine's bedrooms at Versailles. The Lyons area is home to the first Jacquard loom, which was developed there, and the textiles that were produced from this area reached their peak during the 1800's. I have been tracking down special fabrics that were made in different stylistic periods around that time and have seen these fabrics in Paris at Versailles and also at Fontainebleau Chateaus. To see the textiles in their context with the original furnishings is extremely informative and inspiring. Surprisingly, I found that I was able to recall a lot of the French language I had learnt in my early school years and could communicate effectively with the local people.

I continue to teach weaving and textiles at the ANU. In 2005 I was acting Head of Department for the second half of the year. Sabbatical leave from April to July in 2006 enabled me to travel overseas for work and research, and to complete production of the ACT

Arts Creative Fellowship exhibition work.

In 2006 I worked on a silk velvet commission for Government House in Sydney, developing a new design for the upholstery on a number of antique chairs in a three dimensional shaded velvet Waratah design. This has been a demanding process, involving complex technical skill in the intricate process of designing and weaving fine silk velvet. I have travelled to Italy three times so far to weave the samples for this project. It is exciting to be able to make new velvet designs with an Australian theme using traditional techniques in Florence, Italy.

Chris is currently enjoying his work with engineers and designers at Questacon, the National Science and Technology Centre in Canberra, on projects for exhibitions scheduled two years ahead. He also has time in the studio, where he is working on some challenging personal projects. Our three boys are now grown up and so tall that they tower over me. They are studying hard and looking at their future career options.

REFLECTIONS

It is incredible when I look back and think that I had no loom when I came to Australia in 1986, and now I have one of the most unique looms in the world for a hand weaver, as well as a self run studio. In addition, we plan to automate some equipment, because I suffer from a chronic tendonitis injury in my right arm, caused by long-term overuse.

Throughout my life I have constantly felt God's overwhelming support, even when I was tempted to give up because of difficulties. Many people underestimate their creative potential and do not fully explore and use their skills and abilities. Lack of confidence undermines us, but I believe God encourages us to, "give it a go". The only limitations to what we can achieve are the ones we place on ourselves – but if God is with us, why do we do this? I do not have a great deal of self-confidence so I am grateful to God for his ongoing encouragement. I know that a relationship with God is a process of Him making us strong despite our human frailty.

I have been keen to remind God that He promises special blessings to those who have left their home country to live somewhere else! Those encouraging words He placed in my heart many years ago have been fulfilled in the most unexpected and wonderful ways.

I feel passionately that the vast natural resources we have in Australia should be used within Australia to produce uniquely Australian products, rather than exporting our raw materials to other countries and then importing finished products. I believe we need to look at developing our primary resources, such as fine merino wool, into value-added products within Australia. I think that a lot of money has gone into sporting, scientific and technological research but there has been a serious neglect of long term artistic research. The potential benefits to the economic and cultural climate of Australia are significant.

Through prayer, scripture verses and the words of friends, I have been encouraged to continue with my weaving, especially when I have faced adversity, when something has not worked out as I had hoped, or when I have taken a risk. I have learnt how to deal with criticism and to stand up for what I know to be true, and yet maintain a forgiving spirit in the midst of situations.

God has blessed me in so many ways. He has made available all sorts of experiences that I would never have dreamt possible, and has opened doors to some exciting opportunities to travel and to work on special projects. Every time I knock on a door, or tentatively put a feeler out about something, God magnifies it and brings it back almost a hundredfold. The abundant and overflowing personal encouragement I have received from God over the years has been more than a double portion of His blessing in my life.

Jenny and Chris on their wedding day, Somerset, Weston-S-Mare, August 1986.

Jenny, Chris and Ben with Jenny's scarf ready for presentation to the Queen, 2000.

After the presentation to Her Majesty Queen Elizabeth II, Canberra. Official ACT Government gift, 2000.

School photo of the three boys at Emmaus Christian School, Dickson, from left to right, Ben, Tim and David, 2003.

Jenny working at the computerized 32 shaft loom in her studio, Canberra, 2000.

Jenny working cutting Jacquard cards for velvet weaving at Fondazione Arte della Seta Liso, Florence, Italy, 2003

Triplecloths exhibited at Narek Galleries, Tanja, NSW, 2005.

HILARY MORONEY

Hilary burst into my life a few years ago – full of passion and drama. As we have become better acquainted I have been inspired by her quest for healing from the wounds of abuse, divorce and despair, and by her desire to reach out and help others who have also suffered.

Hilary is passionate about prayer and single minded in following her calling and vision. When we first talked about the writing of Australian Women of Grace, she told me that God had already spoken to her heart about this, and her immediate response was to pray with me that it would come to pass. She prayed, I wrote – and here it is!

I have visited the Prayer House in the beautiful surroundings of their country property at Gundaroo, where Hilary and her husband Paul have created a peaceful haven for people to draw aside for respite and prayer.

Hilary has walked through many deep valleys on her journey to wholeness, but along the way some remarkable doors of opportunity have opened to her, in Australia and in many different countries of the world.

Beauty for Ashes

HILARY'S STORY

As I stood by the graveside of my friend in the year of 1994 I realised that she had understood what was really important in this life. She had shared her life and love with others. In the short eighteen months I had known her, she had a great impact on my life.

My friend had suffered quadriplegia because of a near fatal car accident ten years before, and had overcome enormous difficulties with great courage and tenacity, without complaint. She was determined to live, and not just live, but to embrace life. Eventually, despite all odds, she got up and walked. However, not long after this breakthrough she was stricken with breast cancer. While in the last months of her life she had been angry (yes, she had human frailties), she had still exuded an amazing capacity to love, to understand others, to laugh and enjoy life, to see the good and never judge or criticise.

I realised in that moment while I stood beside her graveside, that when everything else is stripped away, living to bless others is what life is really all about. In the midst of her suffering her home had become a sanctuary, a place of fun and love for confused, lonely teenagers in the community. Her example changed their lives and lives on today as a legacy in my own.

I was challenged as to the state of my own heart, the little value I placed on myself, and the little that I felt I could offer to others. As I saw the teenagers throwing flowers onto her coffin and each sharing how she had brought meaning, hope and joy into their lives I wondered, "If I were lying in that coffin what good would anyone have to say about me?" I was suddenly faced with the darkness and hurt, the disappointment and the shattered dreams of my own life, and my desire to escape from it all. I had always hoped to help others, but instead I saw that I had become bitter and resentful, absorbed by my own traumas.

I can remember watching the autumn leaves falling to the ground, looking up to the blue band of the ocean on the horizon and seeing the beauty of creation all around me. Something inside me surged up with a cry, "I want to live. I still have my life. I want to learn to love others. I want to know what it means to be loved, and to love in a really special way. I want to be free from this cage of darkness."

I believe that God heard my cry that day. A new hope emerged in me that out of the mess of my life, potential existed for a different future. I realised in that moment that I couldn't blame anyone else. I couldn't even blame God. All I could do was desire to change within myself. I had seen my friend overcome so many impossible circumstances; I determined I would do the same. Although I had no idea where to start, I set out on a quest.

Now, many years later, as I look back over the tapestry of my life, I am beginning to understand the purpose God has intended through the weaving together of the various strands. What used to be disconnected stories I can now see as important links in the chain of the heritage of my life that make me who I am today.

MY GRANDPARENTS

When I was growing up I was told the story of my maternal grandfather who fought with the British Army in World War I. He was left for dead on the battlefields in France, then miraculously found and rescued. During his convalescence over many months, he became a Christian, and grew determined to gain a scholarship to Oxford to study theology. While he was in hospital he met a nurse who later became his wife. He eventually became an Anglican minister.

During and after World War II and the bombing of London, my grandfather was involved with the rebuilding of churches and the restoration of Coventry Cathedral, which became an international centre for reconciliation, especially between the UK and Germany. He became the Archdeacon of Coventry, and I believe it is no mistake that his daughter, my mother, married my father, a German Jew from Berlin. I can see that who I am, and the diversity of my life's journey, are an outworking of this union.

My grandfather re-married after the death of his first wife, when my mother was eleven years of age. We called my mother's step-mother Shabby Granny because she lived in Shabbington. In fact, she was anything but shabby. She had grown up in the east end of London, but, determined to make something of herself, she became a nanny to aristocratic families living in stately homes. Later Granny became a Magistrate and my grandfather an Archdeacon. She thoroughly enjoyed telling us stories about when she went to the Queen's garden parties.

My sisters and I constantly felt like the poor relations that were an embarrassment to her. Her expertise on drilling children in the Victorian manner of social etiquette was diligently worked out on us, but the loveless-ness with which it was done had a crushing effect on my spirit. One of my uncles was very involved in the Royal family's social set, so I have memories of listening to my grandmother's endless royal stories. However, we loved to eat her delicious meals, and her yummy desserts were a constant source of excitement and great anticipation.

I have wonderful childhood memories of having fun with my grandfather, and I thought he was my friend. However, as with so many other authority figures in my life, I never knew whether to trust him or what mood he would be in at any one time. My later memories of my grandfather were very different. I felt that he didn't like me, and I was painfully aware of him being irritated by me. I remember the feeling of humiliation when he withheld chocolates from me as a punishment at a family pantomime outing to publicly embarrass me. I knew he was a clergyman so I thought that God must think about me the same way my grandfather and my father did.

My father's parents were German Jews who left Hitler's Berlin in 1936. I am so glad they had the determination and courage to heed warnings from their university friends. I have an extract from my grandfather's diary of September tenth 1936, translated by my sister. It records the day he signed all the documents for their property sales to be finalised before he, with my grandmother, their two children and their nanny, left Germany on a train to freedom in Switzerland. Through the help of the underground movement they fled on the pretence of going on a skiing holiday. They carried their wealth with them in a valuable old Bible hidden in a brown paper bag while the family silver was hidden in clothes in their luggage. They sold the Bible to auctioneers in America and were later admitted to the UK as alien status refugees at the beginning of World War II.

Their nanny is one of the main heroes of this story for me. Although not Jewish herself, she travelled with my grandparents to a foreign land, willingly leaving behind her family and friends in Germany. She remained faithful to our family and cared for my grandparents until the end of their lives. As I contemplate her uncomplaining love and generosity to us all, even today, she embodies to me a life of selfless serving, integrity and devotion.

My grandfather committed to establishing his pharmaceutical factory and business to help the British war effort. My grandparents and their children were officially christened as Christians, and the children found their personal faith in Christ at a later stage of their lives. All their working years in the UK my paternal grandparents lived almost as refugees in rented accommodation, not feeling accepted. It appeared that they were unable to integrate or establish a new home and kept their treasures in storage for many years.

Finally, when my grandparents retired, they decided to put down their roots in the land that had given them refuge. They bought and renovated a mansion in Sussex. They were keen gardeners and created wonderful projects, built bridges and landscaped gardens. My grandfather started wood carving and sculpture when he was seventy and surprised us all with his realistic carvings of animals.

My older sisters and I visited them twice a year in Sussex during the school holidays. On these visits most of our time was spent in the nursery with the nanny, or out in the gardens, only seeing our grandparents at meal times. When we visited with my parents for special occasions we saw far more of our grandparents, which I loved. I remember getting dressed up for a ball in the long hall when I was about eight years old. The silver and crystal twinkled under the lights on the long banqueting table, where sculptors and artists from London and the surrounding countryside came and mingled and socialised. I thought I was in heaven. It all seemed so grand and beautiful.

On one occasion during the summer holidays, when I was about twelve and visiting on my own without my older sisters, I tried to protect my fragile grandmother from some dogs that were fighting and I was bitten by their big dog, Chum. I was left abandoned in a dark back room with no pain killers for a few days and was not allowed to phone my parents. I can only imagine this was because my grandparents felt so badly about the incident. Fortunately, my father was called down just in time to attend to my injury, although for a while it was uncertain as to whether I would have to have my leg amputated or not. I remember a number of doctors coming to our house and peering at my badly infected leg.

I had to stay in bed for many weeks, and the district nurse visited and dressed the wound daily. I became very good at putting on bandages. However, I made a full recovery and I thank God that I still have two legs to take me on adventures today. I felt forsaken and abandoned during that experience and decided that I could not trust adults to take care of me. I made an inner vow that in future I would have to take care of myself. In later years I have been healed of this pain of abandonment and have forgiven all concerned.

I passionately loved my grandparents, and I still love the sound of a German accent. Sadly, they never really got over the trauma and loss of their life in Germany, although they were amazing people and maintained their sense of humour throughout their lives. Back then I had no idea of the heartache they had experienced. Those rare fun times we enjoyed on our visits were a taste of the world they had left behind.

GROWING UP

Life was far from easy growing up in our family. I was born in 1957. For years I believed that my arrival in this world was a mistake. This was reinforced by my parents often telling stories of how they had never planned to have me. I was told that once the idea of a third child was accepted, they were hoping for a boy. I was not what they desired or expected. I was the third girl and was named Hilary Vivien after male mountaineers who scaled Mount Everest not long before I was born. Apparently I didn't speak until I was three or four years old, but my friends and family tell me I have made up for it ever since! I grew up confused about my identity, privately dressing up as a princess, but with the public bravado of a tomboy. It has taken years to come to a place of peace within myself and with my identity as a woman.

My father had many struggles throughout his life. I can't even begin to comprehend what it must have been like for him to rise up and overcome the bullying in the school playground of an inner London suburb prior to World War II when he came to England as a German speaking boy from Berlin. The tragic legacy for our family was the resulting emotional, mental and abusive turmoil we experienced in our home. My father worked extremely long hours at the hospital in Oxford in his profession as a doctor. He was recognized for his many achievements in cancer research. Because of the demands of his work my mother found it hard to cope at home.

I admired my father's capacity to care for his patients, which was how I longed for him to care for me. I didn't understand why he was not like this at home. I have memories of seeing him sitting compassionately at the bedside of critically ill patients each Christmas when we went to the ward for Christmas lunch. I loved to go on the ward round with him, and as I stood watching him a longing rose up within me to also reach out to deeply hurting people.

We had very little money, but we children were sent to good schools at great sacrifice on the part of my parents, for which I am deeply grateful. Because I received all the hand-me-down clothes from my sisters this compounded the rejection I felt, and I developed an Orphan Annie mentality. I clearly remember how I yearned for something pretty and new, but it never seemed to come.

We attended the local village church weekly where, sadly, the reality of the gospel was never preached. We had a shell-shocked vicar who stuttered and shouted and read out of other theologian's writings, but rarely read the Bible. After all those years of Sundays I had no idea who Jesus really was, or of his love and power to change us. What a different life I could have led if I had discovered this while I was still young!

On top of the emotionless preaching, when I was nine I was sexually abused by one of the elders of that church. Although I tried to seek help, it was just too hard for people to accept. No-one would listen to or believe me. I felt that nobody cared. From that time on, going to church was a painful experience for me. I couldn't understand why I felt such anger every Sunday. I was frightened by the ancient wall murals of St. George slaying the dragon, which presented a picture of cruelty that resonated with my pain. However I loved singing the hymns, and I remember turning from those frightening walls to my one friend at the church whom I looked forward to seeing every week. Interestingly he was an old German general, and I joined in with him as he sang the hymns in church with all his heart, full of joy and gusto. We would catch each other's eyes, and smile as our spirits met in celebration and worship.

After years of being at home, my mother finally began to achieve her lifelong dream of training at an art school in Oxford. This brought her great fulfilment because she proved to be a gifted artist. However, when she found she was pregnant again she struggled with the realisation that this meant giving up her art classes. The birth of my sister turned out to be a great blessing to the family as she is a wonderful person. She and my parents became very close, with my sister caring for my mother in her later years.

This was a traumatic time for me. I was eleven years old, and until then I had been the baby of the family. Now I felt I had been displaced. This coincided with my starting High School. I waited daily, for what seemed hours, by an old graveyard to catch the bus home after school. I felt lonely and disconnected from my older sisters, whom I loved dearly, because they went to another school. I also felt that I had emotionally lost my mother who found coping with four children, as well as my father's work stress, overwhelming. This led to her suffering with depression over a number of years.

My two older sisters went to a government subsidised selective Grammar school, but because I'd failed the entrance exam I had to go to a girl's public school that had much higher fees (equivalent to a private school in Australia.). This caused much pressure and financial hardship for my parents, for which I felt deeply guilty. During my school days if I only achieved 95% I had to explain to my father what happened to the last 5%. It seemed impossible for me to meet his expectations. I tried so hard to get it right and to be a 'good girl', but sadly I felt I could never win. I was never what he wanted.

The school I attended was run on draconian Victorian lines, but the Head Mistress was an agent of God's grace to me. I spent a lot of time in her study and I thank God to this day that she believed in me. She never shouted or called me an 'odious child' as my step-grandmother did. She just calmly asked me to explain why, when I was capable of doing good things, I had committed the latest attention-seeking prank. This could be any one of a number of things, such as squeezing shoe polish carefully along the window pane lines just ahead of the window cleaners so that as they cleaned it smeared all over the windows and their cloths and hands, giving me a great giggle as I hid behind the coat and bag racks. Both at school and at home I ended up being either the scapegoat or the clown. To deflect negative attention I would engage in amateur theatricals in an endeavor to survive and to keep the peace. It was never safe to be myself.

TEENAGE TRAUMAS

Sadly, my father sought to meet his emotional and physical needs through his relationship with me in my early teenage years. This started after my younger sister was born and went on for a number of years. I remember lying in bed each morning dreading the sound of his footsteps coming down the corridor towards my door and hearing the door handle turning, knowing what was to come. After he left my room I would have to pass my parent's bedroom door on my way to music practice. He would then storm out of his room to attack and berate me verbally.

I was often paralysed with fear as I stood at the top of the stairs with the darkness of the stairwell behind me. Sometimes it was all I could do to keep standing up and not fall down the stairs. This went on for several minutes while he dumped his guilt and frustration on me for some invented excuse, such as my being two minutes late for my music practice. He would not stop attacking me verbally until he had reduced to me to tears and saw that he had overpowered me. This happened day after day and left me deeply confused and emotionally traumatised.

One of the most destructive outcomes of this was that eventually I made an inner vow that I would never again give him the satisfaction of making me cry. And I never did! I realise now, in hindsight, that this was Satan's attempt to destroy me through my father, and I can honestly say that I have now, through the grace of God, completely forgiven him. However, the legacy of a crushed spirit, broken trust and shattered sense of identity was devastating. The way I coped and survived was through disassociation and living in a fantasy world. It is amazing the power of the mind to deny realities that are too painful to face. I was determined to survive and to find goodness in this life, despite all the darkness. Those memories were shut away and emotions stuffed down until I was about thirty six years old, when they started to surface in dreams and flash-backs, as cracks of my denial system crumbled during the traumas of my first marriage.

I had effectively internalized all the grief and anger, like many children do, and as a result developed irritable bowel syndrome. I was determined to escape the misery and pain and to prove that I could do something worthwhile to impress my parents. At thirteen years of age I threw myself into the life of Young Farmers' Clubs that offered fun for young people in country villages, including farm visits, where we had a great time in the outdoors. I'm so grateful to the older members who nurtured and mentored me and taught me that there were possibilities and potential for me in life. I made sure I was involved in 'useful' activities, such as being on the organising committee for dances, performing in shows, training for debating, public speaking and stock judging. Any activity I undertook had to be considered by my father to be educational before I was allowed out of the house.

Tragically, on my confirmation day when I was thirteen years old, one of my uncles plied me with wine and I tottered drunkenly up the aisle of Christ Church Cathedral, Oxford, with a splitting headache. I remember looking along the line of candidates who seemed so sincere and committed, and then at the bishop moving along the line towards me, and thinking, "What is wrong with me? I don't want a strange old man to lay his hands on my head." I didn't like it and did not know why. I am sure now that it was because I was traumatised by the abuse and disconnected from my feelings. Getting dressed up in the white dress and veil, going through the rituals and repeating the prayers seemed such a farce to me.

There were many strange ingredients to my upbringing. There was a total denial of our Jewish heritage so that all the alienating taunts at school about my unusual surname and my olive skin and dark hair didn't make any sense. At home we lived in an angry religious environment. As the Barbara Streisand song says, "I lived in a No you Don't world, overrun with rules". We had little contact with my father. After his initial affectionate greeting to my sisters and me when he returned home from work, he disappeared into his study and shut the door. The only family contact was during the evening meal, when we children were expected to sit in silence while he recounted the happenings of his day. We were not allowed to speak or interrupt. After dinner he helped my mother wash up the dishes and then he worked in his study every evening as well as most weekends.

I escaped into a fantasy world, longing for safety, love and acceptance. I dressed up constantly, dreaming of being an actress in plays, and thirsting for the odd visits to my grandparents' homes. My parents didn't seem to have the inclination to spend time with us, or to make time for visitors. I found comfort in dreaming that one day I might become a famous actress and find Prince Charming who would love and take care of me.

The happiest memories of my childhood are of the holidays, especially our three week family camping holidays, when we drove long distances across Europe into the forests and mountains my father loved. He would take my older sisters and me walking up into the mountains, while my mother stayed at the camp site. I remember the joy of discovering glorious flowers, such as Edelweiss and Alpenrose, that appeared so surprisingly among the rocks high up on the Alps, just as I had read about in the Heidi books I adored. In the kiosk at the top of the mountain we'd sit down to a big feast of Black Forest gateau cake and apple juice, which we never had at home. My father was a diabetic, but felt he could indulge himself on such occasions. He was a different person and so much fun to be with out in the midst of nature and away from the pressures of work and his study.

On one of our camping trips in the mountains of Austria we had to hurriedly pull down our wet tents in the midst of a great storm and were the last car to leave the region and get through. We had to drive over a rickety mountain bridge that was being washed away by tumultuous floods raging down the mountainside. What excitement as we passed through the borders into Italy and down to the Adriatic coast to dry out. I remember being amazed by the glorious sunshine and the size of the peaches, so juicy and sweet, and bigger than the size of your hand. How I loved adventures!

CAREER CHOICES

When I left school I decided to do a Cordon Bleu cookery course in central London, and booked myself into a residential hostel across the road. Can you imagine my distress when I discovered it was actually a nunnery masquerading as a hostel for young people? The living conditions were appalling and the food inedible, including pastry pie and gristle sausages – which made the reality of Oliver Twist's experience at the London poor house run by the church (where he was fed small portions of porridge), come alive. These sisters of mercy used the money we paid them for our meals and accommodation to feed good food to the poor street people who queued up daily at the back door.

I know that one of the main ideals of this institution was charity, but we saw and experienced very little of this. I was grateful that I was studying cookery so that at least I had a delicious meal to eat at lunch time. The hungry ballet students residing with me at the hostel were not so fortunate. One night when there was an underground rail strike and I arrived home after curfew, they shut me out on the streets of Soho with nowhere to stay. The nun's attitude did little to soften the burden of reproach I already held against the church for the abuse I had suffered as a child.

I then worked as a chef in a grand old hotel in the Cotswold's and rebelled morally, longing for love and security, desperate to find myself. I tried to discover some sense of my identity through the eyes of men. I had no idea what I wanted to do with my life: I wanted to be a doctor, but my father had forbidden that because he had seen women doctors getting divorced. I also longed to travel and to be an actress, but my father said that nice girls needed to be 'marriageable material' and didn't do any of those things. So I settled on being a nurse to keep everyone happy.

Nursing training in London had its highs and lows. On the wards, although my organisational skills left a lot to be desired, I loved looking after the patients and they seemed to love me. Watching me fool around was probably a bit of light relief and free entertainment to take their minds off their troubles. I spent a lot of time listening to patients' stories as they poured out their hearts to me. However, I would freeze in panic whenever I saw the Head Sister marching fiercely towards me, realising that it must be five p.m. and time to put the bowel motions in the book for that day.

I loved the heated swimming pool at the hospital and the proximity to the West End shows. My great delight was to whiz down to the theatres on my bike after duty was over, hang around the stage door to pick up cheap returned tickets, and later to see the actors. I saw the most wonderful theatre, ballet and opera there. My friends and I also looked forward to the mornings when we cycled down for sumptuous breakfasts in glamorous hotels. We loved to dress up for these occasions as a fantasy escape after the interminable round of bed pans and drudgery we had endured on night duty. I also enjoyed participating in Christmas concerts with the nursing staff, doctors and medical students. Despite all these activities, my heart was not satisfied.

My midwifery training in 1982 was a turning point in my life. I loved looking after the women and their babies who were in hospital, but who were not sick. It was a relief from the sickness and death that swamped me on the main hospital wards. I had wonderful teachers who were inspirational, committed, and had the capacity to mentor and coach me. I learnt how to teach from their example. Their love, strength, calmness and wisdom inspired me as role models of healthy womanhood. They challenged me to rethink

174

what I was going to do with my life, encouraged me to dream, and to live out that dream. When challenged about university and asked, "Why not do medicine?" I responded, "That is not allowed." I decided to pursue a nursing related subject at university, involving counselling or psychology, but first of all I wanted to travel. And so I did.

QUEST FOR TRUTH

With poor equipment but lots of enthusiasm, I set off around the world with my backpack, on my own for a year, heading overland to Nepal and then down through Asia to Australia. I trekked up into the Himalayas, to the Annapurna Sanctuary, seeking for truth, read books on the religions of the world, toyed with Buddhism but rejected Christianity. Then in Colombo, Sri Lanka, I became sick with a bad abscess on my foot. This was a serious problem because I was alone and carrying a backpack. I remember lying on a bench in a humble surgery with a kind doctor asking me about where I was going while he lanced the abscess for me, until I passed out with the pain. I think he must have been a Christian and prayed for me, because on the plane to Bangkok I had a life changing experience. It was April 1983, and I was twenty six.

It is hard to explain, but during that plane trip I had a vision of Jesus standing before me with a lantern, as in the famous picture - *The Light of the World* by Holman Hunt. I was overwhelmed by the warmth and love of his presence, and by the words I heard him say in my heart: "I have forgiven you for everything you have ever done". I realised that this must be Jesus, and I sensed that he was knocking on the door of my heart. He gently asked me to open the door from the inside. But I couldn't. I was terrified because of the picture I saw of the darkness in my heart. But I felt Jesus tell me He had come to heal all the hurt and pain. Then I felt I could open it, just a chink, and I saw a ray of light enter and pierce the darkness. This triggered a release of such pain that I sobbed for seven hours. Jesus' love was so beautiful, gentle and all encompassing. Every time I think of it or share this precious moment in my life, when the love of God touched and transformed me, I still weep in gratitude.

After this experience it came as a reality shock when I arrived in Bangkok but my backpack did not. I felt all alone in the world with just my tickets, passport and money around my waist, and my camera and a note book. I got on to a bus and had no idea where it was going since no one spoke English. Another English woman got on a few stops later and I asked her if she could help me find somewhere to go to, and advise me what to do. She looked after me and took me back to her hostel, lent me clothes and was an angel in disguise to me. I stayed with her that night and was able to retrieve my backpack from the airport the next day. Then I continued on my travels through South East Asia, becoming acutely aware of the spiritual realities of different cultures and religions, eventually reaching Australia.

Initially I shared my experience of the wonder of Jesus' love with everyone I met. However, when I arrived in Australia I was bombarded by the materialism of western culture and lost my awareness of the presence of God's love, and it became just a vague memory. No-one seemed interested, and no-one was able to tell me more about how to continue in my new-found faith. I started to doubt my experience. It was only on reflection years later that I understood what had happened.

Almost immediately after I arrived in Australia I met a young man who was studying medicine and we started to date. At about the same time my father had a massive heart attack. After a short while I decided to return to the UK to care for my father after he had open heart surgery and to try to build bridges of restoration for our relationship. My father and I had many precious times together. I was determined to love and honour both of my parents, to forgive them for past hurts, and do everything I could to make up for my difficult adolescent behaviour and wrong attitudes towards them. My father was diabetic and found it difficult to eat, and it took him a long time to recover. At the end of a few months his specialist gave him early retirement. Amazingly, he lived for seventeen more years. During this intense time of being a parent to my parents, old pain and confusion started to surface. I didn't know what to do to ease this emotional pain.

I started university at the London School of Economics, studying Sociology, Psychology and Moral

Philosophy. I had a wonderful tutor and felt like Rita in the stage production of Educating Rita, having no idea how to embrace this new world. I was almost writing out the books I read because I did not have the required analytical study skills. Each week my tutor listened to one of my travel stories while we discussed the diversity of cultures I observed, and then set me an essay topic to research on some cultural or sociological theme. I loved it.

After my travel experiences I found it hard to adjust back to life in the UK with the cold weather and much unresolved emotional pain relating to my family. Living in a group house at the back of Clapham stifled my soul, especially on the cold grey days in the never-ending winter, with the endless bus journeys on foggy mornings. In the past I'd been a bicycle ride away from the exciting centre of London's activities. I found it hard to contemplate living in the suburbs with limited finances for the next three years.

RETURN TO AUSTRALIA

My Australian young man came to visit me in London, and nine months later, in August 1984, we were married. We travelled back to Australia through Asia and arrived in Sydney in January 1985. Perhaps this show biz style romance was doomed from the start, since I did not understand the ethnic expectations of my new Italian/Australian family, that the woman would be subservient to the man. Neither of us really knew what it took to build a healthy long term relationship. I was devastated that my marriage could end up in a similar family saga to that of my childhood, with destructive and dysfunctional patterns of relating that were the exact opposite of all my hopes and dreams.

I will be forever grateful for the generosity of my first husband's parents in helping us financially in those early days, and to other friends that welcomed me to Australia. The irony was that, as I began the next three years at university in Sydney, I was given the opportunity to study medicine. My husband was not keen on me doing that so I started an Arts degree in Psychology, doing subsidiary studies in English and Drama, subjects I loved but had never been good at. At the end of the first year I came second in Psychology and was approached to further my academic career in this field. But my heart was not in scientific methods, which were, to me, 'rats and statistics'. I am deeply indebted to my English tutor who helped me to change my focus from attaining high marks in a safe subject to pursue the challenge of gaining skills in essay writing and analysis, to achieve my dream of studying drama, Shakespeare and theatre and to gain a BA in Drama and English.

A group of us set up a University Drama Society, and I was able to pursue my childhood desire of being involved in many drama performances and productions. Eventually I realised that I did not want all the stress and pressure of acting. I enjoyed much more the creative process of helping others to develop their acting skills. With the help of a dear friend I worked toward my Drama Teaching Associate Diploma exams through Trinity College, London, which I passed. This equipped me to teach drama.

My marriage during this time was very stressful because my husband was studying medicine, with all the pressures this involved. We both made some unwise decisions and had unrealistic expectations of each other. We shared very little in common, other than our love of the bush and cooking, because we came from such divergent cultural backgrounds. We went to counselling for a while and tried to work things out. In the end I gave up drama and tried to be a chameleon by changing to fit his expectations, denying more and more of who I was to try to please him. I gave up more and more of my interests. Eventually I became completely lost on the inside. Emotionally, it was just like being back in my childhood home.

After I finished university I went back to nursing as a midwife for some years, as well as part-time teaching communications in a Technical and Further Education (TAFE) College in a major city in New South Wales. I was terrified of even the thought of having children, and of repeating the emotionally painful cycle I had gone through myself. I now realised, thanks in part to my studies, that what I had experienced when my little sister was born were fairly normal behavioural problems, which could have been worked through with a bit of patience and understanding. However, my father had considered it best to separate me from my baby sister. Therefore, I had spent much time in my bedroom away from the family, not even allowed to hold her. The messages I had picked up from this painful experience gave me no confidence to believe that I could be trusted to care for children.

One day, while walking in the local shopping mall, I came upon a distressed toddler who had lost his mother. I picked him up to comfort his shaking, trembling little body and felt him relax into my arms as I reassured him. Then I found his mother. After this, I felt hope that perhaps I could be a responsible and caring mother after all.

In 1989, to my great delight, my son Douglas was born. Then in 1991 I was thrilled when my daughter Lavinia was born. My greatest hope was that the experience of these two precious children would be entirely different from my own, and that they would grow up knowing that they were secure, loved, wanted and cherished. But it didn't work out that way. Sadly, they also experienced feelings of rejection, anger and abandonment during their childhood, as is so often the case when cycles of pain are repeated through families. Although it has been a traumatic journey I believe the children are progressively coming through these experiences to growth and maturity by God's grace.

At a church holiday camp in 1993, in a moment of seclusion and quiet, I opened a Bible and felt God speak to my heart through two verses of scripture in Exodus 20:5-6. These verses state that the sins of the fathers who have not loved God will be passed down to the third and fourth generations, but gave a promise of blessing and hope for those who turn back to God, for his love and blessings to flow for a thousand generations to those who love God and keep his commands. I asked God that day to save my children, to save our marriage, and to bring me back to Him.

When Douglas was still a baby I started to attend church at a neighbour's invitation and found joy in singing in the choir. One day, on the spur of the moment, I decided I would visit the Conservatorium of Music in our city, having heard that it was possible to complete my Australian drama qualifications there. I imagined that I would have to pass Australian exams in order to maximise opportunities for teaching in Australia.

I shall never forget that morning when, with my baby on my hip, dressed in a baggy old jumper, I was shown into the office of the Director of the Conservatorium and to my surprise found he was the organist in the church I had just started attending! He was so gracious to me when I apologised for such an impromptu visit, and asked me about my qualifications and experience. He wanted to know about my vision to teach children drama, to release their imaginative potential and creativity through improvisation and voice work.

To my surprise, the Director said that he was looking for someone like me to come and teach at the Conservatorium, and further stated that I was well qualified with my drama degree and Associate

Teaching Diploma from London, and that I could finish my Australian Diploma in my own time. One of the hardest things the Director asked me to do was to go home and write down the concept of what we had talked about to present before the University Board. I believe it was God who placed me in that job, which helped me through the really dark times to come. It was rewarding to teach young children, including many with speech impediments or partial deafness, and to see their self-esteem and confidence rise, with so many going on to achieve excellent examination results. I also enjoyed teaching adults from the corporate world to discover the joys of literature and dramatic expression, as well as training young people to be actors.

The blessings of my children and my teaching made the next six years bitter-sweet. The experience of motherhood was a great joy, but sadly the backdrop of much of our marriage was a repeat of the old abusive cycles I had known in my own family. With hindsight, I can understand that sadly this is so often the case. We take our resentments, emotional wounding and low self-esteem into our relationships, so that the painful cycle continues.

After Douglas was born, my parents came to Australia on a visit and this was such a happy time, when many of my childhood hopes for the restoration of good relationships with my parents seemed to be realised. Out of his home environment my father relaxed and enjoyed life and freedom in the Australian bush. I got to know him in a way I had never been able to before. I was sad when they left to go home.

In 1991, when my father-in-law's health seriously deteriorated, my husband found this situation very hard to cope with, which caused greater stress in our relationship. This was exacerbated by the extremely long hours he worked, holding down two jobs. Sadly, I found myself back in a similar scenario to that which I had experienced in my teenage years with my father. I tried hard to cook my husband wonderful meals, but no matter what I did, it triggered within him violent outbursts of anger. Without any family support of my own, my stress overload increased until I remember standing at the washing machine one day with the pile of children's clothes to be washed beside me, unable to think of what I was meant to do. Something inside me clicked, and I realised that if things did not change soon I was in serious trouble.

TURNING POINT

By 1994 I was crying out to God to forgive me for turning away from Him. My desire was that I might experience what it meant to be loved by Him and by others, and also for me to have the capacity to love and forgive. I asked God to reveal Himself to me and give me a second chance. On the first of January 1995 I hit rock bottom. I went to a Charismatic style church for the first time in my life and recommitted my life to Jesus to serve Him wholeheartedly and to fulfil the destiny for which He had put me on this earth. I surrendered every aspect of my life to Him as my Lord and Saviour. I was baptized in water and the Spirit and felt I had come home at last.

Less than three weeks later my husband left me, shortly after his father's death, which had deeply affected him. It was as if he wanted to live his own independent life, and at that point there seemed no possibility of reconciliation. He continued to come to visit the children for many months while we attempted to work out our differences, but in the end he chose a different path.

From the time of my recommitment, God began to heal my life and the lives of my two children. I attended the local Bible College part-time as well as many teaching workshops, and was mentored by wonderful people. My family in the UK did not know how to cope with my marriage breakup, so my father cut off contact with me. Without family support in Australia, with two young children and not knowing what our future held, I felt forsaken and forgotten. One day, while hanging up the children's washing, I had a strong sense of God speaking to my heart that in the future I would minister healing to His leaders and pastors. That seemed a ridiculous idea at the time, especially when I had so many problems relating to men, but amazingly that is part of what I am doing today.

In 1995 the Lord brought some very kind and understanding Aboriginal Christian pastors across my path to start my journey to the inner healing that I so needed. Somehow, although I found it almost impossible to trust white men at that time, I could trust these gentle indigenous people who had suffered, yet forgiven. These indigenous pastors were like spiritual fathers to me, from whom I learned so much, and whose example has greatly impacted on my life.

In 1996, at the Illawarra Performing Arts Centre, I had the opportunity to present the Christian message through drama to the community. I co-wrote and directed '*Crown of Thorns*', a production about the passion of Christ. It was performed the week before Easter. During this time my children enjoyed spending time with various families in the church. Directing that production I learned to pray out of total desperation, as many times when we turned up for rehearsals in a burnt out, old movie theatre, I felt overwhelmed at having thirty seven actors looking expectantly to me for direction. We held hands and asked God to give us creative ideas, and He did. Many people contributed in different ways and so often, after we prayed, we had a great scene happening!

It was an amazing time of learning to be led by the Spirit of God, as well as to trust and submit to godly church leadership. Only one member of the cast was professionally trained; the rest came out of the fringes of the church and the pub. Many were so touched by working through the gospel stories of the life of Jesus for three months that they had a personal encounter with Christ. In the rehearsals I felt like David might have in the Biblical story when men from all walks of life came to him where he was hiding in the cave of Adullam. He brought them together, formed them into a mighty army, which was skilled and disciplined, and won many battles. Through involvement with the production of *'Crown of Thorns'* people were empowered and equipped to share the good news of the gospel with others. I loved it, thinking at last I had discovered what I could do for God and His people in the area of the creative arts. However, as it turned out, God had other plans for me.

During my time of singleness the children and I had prayed every night that God would prepare and bring a kind and godly husband and step-father into our lives, but deep in my heart I secretly hoped it would not be too soon. However, I trusted and thanked God that it would come about in His perfect way and time, and determined that I would not try to make it happen. What an irony to discover that this new adventure was just around the corner, and that God was already preparing someone's heart to be able to love us.

PAUL

After the production finished on Easter Saturday, a friend had asked me to video her daughter's wedding at a church in Canberra. This occurred only four days after my divorce had come through in 1996. It was here that God literally collided me with Paul, when my friend Ruby introduced us. We both knew that our meeting was a God-ordained encounter, even though I didn't know how to trust a man, and was only just learning to trust God. This was the biggest faith journey of my life. As we shared our vision and calling we believed that God had brought us together. Paul's wife had died not long before in 1995, but he was prepared to take on a new family. We were married in Gundaroo on January eighteenth 1997, and the children were included in the prayers after we took our wedding vows.

Many people ask me how God can bless a second marriage when it says in the Bible that God hates divorce. My understanding is that God, through the sacrifice of Jesus on the cross, is gracious to all people who genuinely repent of their sins and forgive others. He forgives them. There are many instances in the Bible where God gave people a second chance to fulfil his purposes. This has been our experience. I appreciate the definition of redemption my pastor gave me when I was despairing whether God could ever use me because of my past. My pastor explained that when Jesus redeems a situation, in His grace He turns the situation around and makes it something better than it was in the first place. I have found this to be true in my life.

There were many adjustments for Paul and me to make, and for the children, when we moved to live in Gundaroo, a small country town half an hour north of Canberra. But God was gracious to us during this time of adjustment, particularly as I worked through deep emotional upheavals. Many times people go through long seasons of healing before they remarry.

In the case of Paul and me it would appear that we were a work in progress, and the Lord put us together in our brokenness to be a major part of each other's healing. It is such a joy to now be able to help others with similar issues.

I believe that life is a journey of walking towards wholeness and discovering the unique identity and purpose that God has created for each one of us. The gift of free choice, given to us by God, brings with it the ability to make wrong choices as well as right ones. Sadly, for many of us our bad decisions create emotional and spiritual obstacles that obscure our paths, and these need to be cleared away. I think back with awe at the ways God has orchestrated times of deep inner healing in my life.

THE PRAYER HOUSE

In the early days at Gundaroo it was a real challenge to understand my calling to intercession and prayer. I had hoped to pursue the creative arts I loved, but it was not to be at that time. One day in worship, during the time Paul and I were engaged to be married, God gave me a vision to build a Prayer House on the acre of land at Gundaroo. When I shared this with Paul, he told me this had also been the dream of his first wife before she died, and he was thrilled it was now going to be fulfilled. I had no idea how this would work out, in fact I was happy to clean the toilets and wait for someone else to come and handle the spiritual side of things. However, that was not the plan that God showed us. This vision was realised when we built a separate cottage on our property for people to come to stay, rest, pray and worship.

In June 1998 the Prayer House was dedicated to God as a place where His healing grace could be experienced, just prior to a British prayer team coming out to Australia, to bring spiritual closure for past wrongs between our nations, including the convict issues. That was the beginning of my involvement with prayer for the nations, in partnership with the indigenous people. The British prayer leaders handed the mandate on to the Australian Prayer Network for us to pray for God's destiny to be fulfilled in Australia. I felt God ask me to commit myself to pray for Australia.

The calling and vision I received was to pray for the reconciliation of people to God, and people to each other, and for me to be a bridge builder between people groups. This vision flowed out of my experience when I attended the International Reconciliation Coalition gathering for prayer in New Zealand in February 1999. This was led by John Dawson, together with many Christian leaders, including Aboriginal and Maori delegates. It was an important time of dis-covering God's unfolding plan for me and the Prayer House Ministry, when I met many key prayer leaders, with whom I have had a continued association in our desire to see Australia enter into the fullness of her destiny. These people are very precious to me.

On my return from New Zealand a group of women met with me regularly over a period of several months at the Prayer House to pray for Australia. It was with these women that I really learnt how to pray and to understand God's heart for the people of Australia. As a culmination to this season of prayer I attended the national gathering of reconciliation and repentance at Uluru in Central Australia in July. Christians from all over Australia, including many indigenous people, prayed for God to have mercy on our nation and to heal our land.

From this flowed an invitation for Paul and me to join the Australian Prayer Network delegation of prayer leaders, including indigenous pastors, to the UK in September 1999. This was a journey of forgiveness to bless Britain in response to the earlier visit of the British prayer team to Australia. During this time God called me to stand in the gap in prayer on the basis of my Jewish heritage, and by His grace, while we were in the UK, He also brought healing between my father, me and Paul. This was especially meaningful because my father died three months later, in February 2000.

Following my father's death I experienced a period of grieving and healing, which included a visit to Germany, the land of my father's birth. Paul and I and the children had a wonderful time as we discovered the beauties of Berlin, my father's birthplace, and we imagined how my grandparents, in years past, would have walked along the grand old streets of this great city. We also had the privilege of attending and praying with a small home fellowship group in Berlin, where some beautiful German Christians ministered to us all.

We shared our family story with them and they wept as they prayed for us to be released from any of the negativity that had surrounded the Jews who had been forced to leave Germany prior to World War II.

After this, as a family we attended the Gideon's Army II gathering in Hanover to pray for Europe, as part of the Australian Prayer Network team. For the children this was a living geography lesson, as people representing nations from western and eastern Europe met together, shared their stories, and prayed for a better future.

We then travelled to the UK, where Douglas and Lavinia stayed with my family and became better acquainted. Meanwhile, Paul and I participated in a prayer tour of Ireland, exploring Paul's heritage, and discovering the roots of Irish Christianity, which have formed an important part of our cultural heritage in Australia. We heard stories of the grinding poverty that so many Irish people experienced, which forced them to migrate to Australia to take up a new life. It was inspiring to hear of ordinary people who had risen above the disadvantages of their past. The legacy of many Irish settlers, who championed values of justice, mateship, and giving people a fair go, lives on in Australia today.

An important realisation that came out of these journeys was that around the world, twenty-four-hour centres of prayer and worship were being established in an unprecedented way. This resonated with our vision to see Prayer Houses established in Australia and many nations, and our desire to see continuous prayer and worship established in Canberra.

The Prayer House Ministry became linked into the vision of the World Wide Prayer Watch Network in Jerusalem, where representatives from nations around the world go up to Jerusalem each year for the All Nations Prayer Convocation, to pray for Arab and Jewish reconciliation, for Israel and the Middle East, and for all the nations of the world. The key scripture of our Prayer House ministry is Isaiah 35, which speaks of healing and restoration, and of the people from the nations going up to worship in Jerusalem. This became a reality in my life between 2000-2002 when I joined the Australian delegation to Jerusalem. The experience challenged many of my deeply held anti-Sematic views, which came from a family that denied our Jewish heritage. I had to confront the stigma I had felt as a child with Jewish ancestry, growing up in an alienating school culture. What a work of grace God has done in my life to soften my heart, and to bring compassion to pray for the Jewish people through these difficult times. Out of relationships formed there, I then went on to pray in Singapore with people from the nations of South East Asia and the South Pacific on two separate occasions.

Douglas, Lavinia and I enjoyed an exciting adventure in July 2002. We were part of an Australian mission team who visited an orphan childrens' camp in Vladivostok, Russia, for two weeks. It was wonderful to see the children in the camps respond to God's love expressed through the team. We took many gifts with us and, as well as teaching them Bible stories, we taught them about the flora and fauna of Australia. They were delighted at the idea of platypuses and kangaroos. They had so little and were excited at receiving their gifts, but they especially treasured the Bibles that we gave to them. Our family continues to pray for these children.

The Prayer House was incorporated on the 29th September 2003, exactly three years to the day of my first arrival in Jerusalem. Since that time there has been an intensified focus on praying for God's purposes to be established in Canberra, and particularly for righteousness in the Parliament and governments of our nation. We are gradually discovering more of the calling of Prayer House Ministries Australia, including giving support to indigenous missions.

At a Parliamentary Prayer Breakfast in 2005, I had the great privilege of meeting a wonderful Arab Christian, General George Sada, a retired Iraqi General who served under Saddam Hussein. He had amazing stories to tell of how God had protected him when he refused to obey orders that would have caused mass destruction. He also told how thousands of Iraqis are publicly identifying themselves as new followers of Christ, many of whom converted because Jesus appeared to them in dreams or visions. What a healing moment it was in my life when, on being told of my Jewish heritage, he hugged me and said "I am your brother, you are my sister; we are one in Christ". We prayed together for Jewish/Arab reconciliation.

MILESTONES

On looking back over the years, I can now see the fulfilment of the dream that was born in my heart when I stood beside the grave of my dear friend in 1994. It is one of the greatest joys of my life that through giving hospitality in the Prayer House on our beautiful country property we are able to minister to the many people God sends to us. It is a constant source of wonder to me to spend many hours sitting and praying with people and seeing God mend broken hearts and lives.

Over the years from 1997 I studied at Unity Bible College, and finally completed Diplomas in both Theology and Ministry in 2006. Although it took me a long time to complete my studies, one subject at a time, I persevered – obtaining the dubious title of the most long-standing student at Unity College. I hope that this is an encouragement to others to press on regardless of how long it takes. We might be like the tortoise compared to the hare, but we get there in the end.

Part of my involvement with Unity College has included praying with others with a similar vision, to see the creative arts released across the church in Australia and the nations. This has sprung from my passion to see young people in Australia released into their potential through drama, and for them to experience creative ways to share the Christian message in a manner that is culturally relevant in today's society.

From the year 2000 I worked on my Wagner Leadership training from the Wagner Leadership

Institute at Colorado Springs in the USA, attaining my Doctorate in Practical Church Ministry in December 2005. On this journey into the Bible, God's word to us, I have felt that I have been attending the school of the Holy Spirit, and it has been a journey into freedom.

In November 2004 I met with Pastor Danny Nalliah from Catch the Fire Ministry in Melbourne, Victoria, and offered to become the Canberra coordinator for the Rise Up Australia prayer movement that he has initiated in cities across this nation. Pastor Danny is a man with great courage, who has stood up for freedom of speech and the liberty to preach the undiluted truths of Christianity in Australia. This has been at great personal cost, to the extent of him being taken to court and facing the possibility of imprisonment. Working under his leadership has caused me to grow in my faith, and to face my fears of persecution in the future. I have been encouraged that more and more people are coming together to pray, often on a monthly basis, particularly in the light of the catastrophic world events that are unfolding every day.

How wonderful it was in 2005 to travel to the UK again with Lavinia for a family wedding, and to at last feel that I belonged. This transformation has come from the progressive healing of my broken spirit and the wounds of my heart. It has been a long and painful journey of prayer, walking with the Lord through the valleys of abuse, divorce and despair. Back with my family again, free from the old pain triggers, I felt at peace. It was so refreshing to experience relationships with my sisters and family members on a new level of maturity, love, and acceptance of each other that I had never previously dreamed to be possible. It was also encouraging to see the answers to many of my prayers.

At the end of June 2006 the Prayer House entered into its eighth year of ministry, a time of new beginnings focusing on worship and prayer in preparation for the return of the Lord. In September 2006 I am part of a team going to Jerusalem to worship the Lord in unity and reconciliation. The team is led by indigenous leaders from Australia and the South Pacific Islands (the Bethany Gate nations as they are known to prayer leaders).

REFLECTIONS

I am realising at last that I have permission to be me, the unique person God has created, no longer fearful of other people's disapproval. I have also found that now I have far more love to give out to others. The hardest person to forgive is myself. Experiencing the generosity and loving kindness of my family and friends has been an important part of this healing journey.

I wait with great anticipation to discover the new direction that I sense my life is about to take, to enter into the purpose that the Lord has prepared me for in this next chapter of my life. Despite the challenges and hard times, I could never have believed this adventure of following the Lord would be so stimulating, satisfying and exciting!

As a world traveller I have experienced many of the religions, cultures and diversities of this planet. As a nurse and midwife I have experienced the highs and lows of the miraculous events surrounding birth and death. As a drama student and teacher I have studied in depth the wisdom of such sages as William Shakespeare. And as a wife and mother I have experienced the joy and hurts of close love relationships. None of these things, precious as they are, were able to heal my broken heart or satisfy the deep inner longing of my soul.

Now I have become an avid student of the Bible, and through this I have experienced the power of God's love and His presence to heal and bring restoration to my body, soul and spirit. This is the foundation that brings joy to all the other aspects of my life. As the title of my story says, He has given me "... *a crown of beauty instead of ashes, the oil of gladness instead of mourning, and a garment of praise instead of a spirit of despair." Isaiah 61:3 (NIV)*

I am convinced that beyond the humdrum and mediocrity of every day life, beyond the beauty of creation, the excitement of holidays, the joys of reunions, the thrills of success and celebrations, the darkness of violation, despair and separation, there lies a whole other dimension of spiritual reality, of oneness, communion and intimacy with God. To be able to spend one's life sharing with others the knowledge of the saving grace and love of God brings true fulfilment.

Hilary at 17 years of age as bridesmaid for her eldest sister.

Hilary at her graduation from University of NSW, April 1988.

The Prayer House, Gundaroo

Hilary and Paul with Douglas and Lavinia.

Hilary (in centre of picture holding banner) at the "Opening The Nations' Gates" Conference in the Federal Parliament, July 2004.

Hilary at the "Uluru Healing the Land Conference", July 2005.

Hilary and General George Sada, an Arab Christian from Iraq, at Parliamentary Prayer Breakfast, 2005.

ROBYN HIPKISS

At first I wasn't going to include my story. I felt that it was perhaps not exciting or dramatic enough to be interesting. However, I felt that I could not ask others to do something I was not prepared to do myself.

To my surprise, the writing of my own story became a journey of re-discovering who I was. In coping with situations along the way it seemed that I had almost lost sight of my own identity. In the process of writing, something has been restored that I had lost. I have gained a greater understanding and perspective of my life.

Living with cancer and major surgery has taught me that every day we have on this earth is a gift from God to be treasured and enjoyed. Being a Christian is not an automatic guarantee of freedom from pain and suffering, but the wisdom we gain from our experiences of life can be shared with others in similar situations to encourage them on their journey.

Sustaining Grace

ROBYN'S STORY

There was great excitement in my home town, the small seaside town of Victor Harbour in South Australia. In fact, there was great excitement all over the countryside because Billy Graham was coming to hold an Australia-wide Crusade. It was 1958, and land lines had been set up to relay his messages to country towns so people could go to designated locations and listen while his message was broadcast over the loudspeakers. This was a huge project, and many churches and technicians combined their efforts to make it happen. I was home from Adelaide for the weekend and a friend and I decided to go. The church was packed out, so we sat in the car outside, along with many others, and listened to Billy Graham preach with great authority and passion. My heart was deeply stirred by his words and I resolved to go to his Crusade in Adelaide to hear more from this inspiring preacher. Little did I know that this was to be the beginning of a new and wonderful chapter of my life.

HOW IT ALL BEGAN

My parent's love story could have been taken from the pages of a popular romantic novel. My mother grew up on the Broadwater, a property in Busselton, Western Australia. My grandmother, known to us as Granny Packard, had aspirations for her daughter to meet a distinguished young English gentleman with good prospects, so she sent Betty on a one way ticket to the United Kingdom when she was eighteen years of age to live with my great-grandfather, Sir Edward Packard, and his family. Betty had a great trip over with all the fun of shipboard life, and while in the UK had a wonderful time meeting aunts and cousins and socialising with all their friends. However, Granny Packard had not counted on the considerable charm and gifted writing skills of young Wilfred Butler, a humble bank clerk, whom Betty had met before she left Australia.

Betty and Wilfred corresponded faithfully for four years, and when he proposed by letter she accepted by return cable. My mother then got a job and saved up enough money to pay for her return ticket to Australia. Six weeks after her arrival back from the UK, in October 1934, they were married. Their love story endured through the years, and they did live happily ever after, despite some great hardships. These included the tragic death of their dearly loved first born son Tony, at two years of age, through a doctor's negligence; their fifth child, Jocelyn, born with Downes Syndrome; and Dad's ongoing serious health problems that included Meniere's disease, two bouts of tuberculosis, and emphysema.

If you were to judge by today's standards, our family had few of the things deemed essential by many for a successful family life, such as wealth and possessions. Despite this, my parents had an abundance of the most important thing in life – their deep and enduring love and commitment to one another and to their family. We might have been poor financially, but we were rich in love. Every day Dad told Mum how much he loved her as well as encouraging and affirming us children. This created a loving environment in our home and my childhood memories reflect that happiness.

Although the memories are hazy, they are warm and comforting. As I think back over the years those memories come to life, like particles floating in the air, unseen and not thought about until a shaft of sunlight catches them in a darkened room, and suddenly there they are. I remember the comfort of snuggling up on my father's lap as he soothingly stroked my hair and tucked it behind my ear; lazy summer days spent playing by the grass tennis courts while my parents enjoyed a relaxed game of social tennis with their friends; bed time stories told by my Dad with such drama and suspense it fired our imagination and left us excited and unable to sleep for hours; family meal times a babble of voices and laughter with everyone trying to talk at once; and that memorable day in 1945 when we lived in Kingscote on Kangaroo Island and peace was declared at the end of World War II. It was a great occasion and the whole town went wild with excitement. People congregated in the main street cheering, shouting, singing, blowing whistles and dancing the hokey pokey. At five years of age I was too young to understand why, but I felt the joy and shared the excitement.

OUR GREAT ADVENTURE

Like many people, Dad had a dream. Although he was a town dweller and a bank manager he dreamed of becoming a farmer and living on the land. Mum had always been a country girl at heart. We were living in the country town of Kadina, a few hours north of Adelaide in South Australia, when the bank indicated that a posting to Sydney was imminent. City living held no appeal for them so my parents decided it was time to follow their dream and begin actively looking for a farm. The whole family became involved when we put up a big poster and stuck pictures all over it of all the things we would like on our dream farm.

The budget was limited, but eventually we found a small property at Inman Valley in the south of the state. Dad resigned from the bank, and in 1950 we embarked on our great adventure. Our farm consisted of a modest 200 acres (80 hectares), a humble home without any running water or electricity, a corrugated iron lean-to bathroom with a roaring chip heater, and a hole-in-the-ground toilet that was situated a considerable distance from the house. As the farm didn't produce much, apart from the numerous rabbits that ate everything that was planted, Mum became an expert on cooking rabbit. We existed on rabbit stew, fricassee rabbit, baked rabbit and rabbit casserole, cooked on a wood burning stove, along with home grown vegetables, eggs from the chooks, and the dairy produce from a few cows. We survived and we thrived!

This transition from a comfortable and secure life with Dad's career in the bank to the hazards of farming and rural living was a fabulous time for us children, but proved to be a financial disaster for Mum and Dad. With five children to feed there was very little to go around. We had one set of clothes on, and one set in the wash. We children experienced the wonderful freedom of living in the country, riding our horses around country tracks, getting to know the other children in the area, and exploring through the bush. We didn't have any of the proper equipment for horse riding such as saddles or helmets, but rode bareback with old bridles and bits of rope for reins.

To go to school we had to leave home early in the morning, walk three kilometres down an old bush track and then take a bus for sixteen kilometres in to the school. In the winter we got up by candlelight – it was dark when we left home in the morning and dark again when we came home in the evening. Many nights were spent bent over our school books completing homework assignments by the light of kerosene lamps and candles.

Dad was not mechanically inclined. One day he decided to purchase a second hand tractor to help with the farm work. He drove it home, roaring and shaking so much that it nearly shook him off the seat, parked it in the shed, and it never went again. So much for our venture into mechanisation! Mum and Dad worked hard trying to survive on the farm, but unfortunately Dad's health deteriorated and they had to sell up and move the family in to Victor Harbour, the small, seaside country town where we attended school. The only job my father could find was selling insurance. However, because he was more concerned about giving people all the information they needed than pushing them into signing on the dotted line, he did not make many sales.

Eventually Dad had to go to Adelaide to obtain work, where he secured a job in the Public Trustees Office. Since we could not sell the house at Victor Harbour he commuted every week, boarding at lodgings from Monday to Friday, and coming home on weekends. It was hard for him to be separated from his family.

Sadly, within about eighteen months (in the late 1950s), he developed full-blown tuberculosis and went to Bedford Park Sanatorium for treatment for two years, while Mum coped at home with five children on a small pension. When Dad was cured of the disease he had to continue to commute each week to Adelaide because all efforts to sell the house at Victor Harbour were fruitless. Altogether this continued for seven years and was an extremely difficult time for them, but particularly hard for Mum because we were teenagers by this time and presented many challenges. Finally, to their great relief, the house was sold and the remainder of the family moved to Adelaide.

FINDING FULFILMENT

At fifteen years of age, during my fourth year of High School, I left school to take up a secretarial position in an office in Victor Harbour. Work was difficult to find in a small country town, so my parents felt that I should take this opportunity rather than continue with my studies to obtain my Leaving Certificate. Two of the highlights of my teenage years were completing a modelling course, and making my debut. The modelling Graduation night, and the Debutante Ball were special events when we dressed up and felt like a million dollars. However, in my heart there was an emptiness – I felt that my life had no purpose or meaning. I loved dancing, especially ballroom and rock'n'roll, which my friends and I enjoyed each week at the Saturday night dance at the Wonderland Ballroom. After the dance I would go home and think, "There has to be more to life than this." I attended a denominational church with my family during my younger years, and although at that time the church teachings did not seem particularly relevant to my life, perhaps seeds of truth were sown in my heart that bore fruit in later years.

In 1958, when I was eighteen years of age and had moved to live and work in Adelaide, I attended the Billy Graham Crusade and heard him present the Christian life as one of a personal relationship with God, a life of fulfilment and excitement. At the conclusion of the meeting the huge crowd of people stood to their feet and began to sing that stirring old hymn, "*Just as I am, without one plea, but that Thy blood was shed for me, And that Thou bidst me come to Thee, O Lamb of God, I come, I come*". I felt the Holy Spirit tugging at my heart and calling me to come. With tears streaming down my face I joined the hundreds of others who responded to the challenge that night to come forward and invite Jesus to be their Lord and Saviour. My life was changed from that day onward.

I had come into a personal relationship with God. I knew that He was real and that He loved and cared for me. That well-loved scripture found in John 3:16 became a reality in my life: *"For God so loved the world that He gave His one and only Son, that whosoever believes in Him shall not perish but have eternal life"* (NIV). All my uncertainty and doubts about eternity were gone. My life had gained purpose and meaning. I began to attend a Charismatic church and was delighted by the power and vitality of the services, the loving relationships amongst the people, and the life-giving teaching that I found there. It was certainly not boring! Hundreds of people met every Sunday in old Crusade Hall in the city with its wooden floors and hard, upright wooden chairs. It was not built for comfort, but the walls reverberated with the sound of the people worshipping God, singing with great fervour some of the grand old hymns such as How Great Thou Art, and Blessed Assurance. Many healing miracles took place under the anointed ministry of Leo Harris, the senior pastor of the church. One young man with tuberculosis, who had been given only six weeks to live, was instantly healed, and another woman received perfect hearing in an ear with no ear-drum. People's lives were touched and changed by the power of God in remarkable ways.

I was filled with love for God and wanted to serve him. I was baptized in water and filled with the Holy Spirit. The Bible came alive for me as I began to read it and discover that it contained practical guidelines for living that made good sense. I learned that it is healthy to forgive, that faith can replace fear, that love can overcome hatred, and that God is vitally interested in our everyday lives and will give us wisdom and guidance if we just ask him.

In my early twenties I attended Crusade Bible College four nights a week for two years. This was a time when I soaked up practical knowledge that would equip me for the challenges of life as well as learning answers to my questions about eternal things. I was thirsty for the words of life. While in Bible College I changed jobs and became secretary to Leo Harris, working in the church office for ten years. It was a varied and interesting job that I loved. He was a powerful man with great integrity, faith and vision, but he was also compassionate and kind-hearted. I counted it a privilege to work for him. Leo Harris wrote and published a number of books, which I took down in shorthand and transcribed for publishing, as well as reams of lecture notes. I typed his radio broadcasts while he paced up and down the office behind me, preaching to an unseen congregation. Another of my jobs was to help prepare the newspaper advertisements for the services each week, perhaps foreshadowing my future job of working in advertising at The Canberra Times. The office was the headquarters for all the churches in our denomination so I had a lot of contact with the pastors in our country churches and endeavoured to encourage them in their sometimes difficult and demanding roles.

I prayed that God would bring my future husband into my life, but in the meantime my involvement in Bible College, weekend youth work and children's ministry kept me busy and I loved every minute of it. I formed deep and lasting friendships and appreciated the genuine care and respect the young people had for one another as well as just having fun together. People often said to me, "Mr Right is just around the corner." To which I responded, "Yes, that's all very well, but which corner, and who is he round the corner with?"

Late one afternoon when I was driving home from work, I had a remarkable experience of God's protection. I was in my car, which was stationary in the middle of the road with the indicator on, waiting for oncoming traffic to clear before I could turn right. I glanced in the rear vision mirror, saw a car coming up behind me at high speed and thought, "Wow, he is really moving fast. He must be going straight ahead." The next moment I heard a loud explosion as he slammed into the back of my car and propelled it forward into the path of a car coming towards me, which rammed into the front. I can remember hearing my voice calling out to God to protect me, and feeling no fear, just the peace of His presence in the car, as I was launched out of my seat (there were no seat belts in 1961) to land crumpled underneath the front dashboard on the passenger side of the vehicle. Some passers-by called the ambulance and the officers managed to extricate me from the car, which was a complete wreck. The ambulance took me to the hospital for treatment, where the doctors found, to their amazement, that my only injuries were slight concussion and a deep gash on my knee. I believe this was a truly miraculous escape from serious injury.

CADET CRUSADERS

When I finished Bible College I became concerned that there was no youth group for the eight to twelve year old youth in our church. I went around asking people if they felt a concern too, and if so, wouldn't they like to do something about it? Although many people were interested no-one felt a need to do anything about it except me. I thought, "What can I do? I have no training in teaching or children's ministry?" I asked the advice of other mature Christians. They agreed that I wasn't trained or equipped to do anything of this nature and said it would be foolish to even try. However, my desire and concern would not go away. My pastor encouraged me and said, "What have you got to lose? Why don't you have a go? It is better to have tried and failed than never to have tried at all."

I nervously announced a meeting for parents and children to see if there was an interest in such an undertaking and, not being a woman of great faith, set out just twenty chairs. To my surprise fifty people turned up. A lady volunteered to play the music, others offered to help, and so Cadet Crusaders began. I adapted material from America, with permission, to Australian terminology and conditions, where children could earn badges and advance in rank by learning scriptures, completing assignments on Christian doctrine and living and achieving personal goals. We trained the children in many practical subjects such as public speaking, etiquette and life skills, as well as foundational scriptural truths.

In the fifteen years that it ran, the programme was taken up by a number of other churches around South Australia and also interstate. We saw some wonderful things happen in the lives of these young people. About forty or fifty children attended the weekly meetings, and many of these came to a personal relationship with God, were filled with the Spirit, gained an understanding of the Bible and God's plan for them, and were settled and established in their lives before the pressure of the teen years. Plus they had a lot of fun and formed good friendships along the way.

Weekend activities with bush walks, bonfires and barbecues, swimming outings, scavenger hunts and hay rides gave the city children lots of exposure to the outdoor and country life, which they thoroughly enjoyed. I am so thankful to God that we had no traumas or injuries during this whole time, which was fortuitous considering the large number of children we catered for, with few workers.

We ran camps for children, some of them in primitive conditions. At one Easter Camp at a showground in the Adelaide hills, we had one hundred and twenty children between eight to twelve years of age sleeping in huge marquees. Over the weekend it poured with rain, and I can remember lying on my camp stretcher while various articles of clothing floated past underneath on the stream of water that flowed through the tent. But we survived, and had heaps of fun. We experienced the presence and power of God during those camps, and children's lives were changed. Latent artistic talent and doubtful acting abilities were discovered through the hilarious camp concerts. Years later I have met a number of the children who were in the Cadet Crusaders and who are now adults with their own families. Many gave me such positive feedback about how much they valued their time in Cadet Crusaders.

You never know what God will do through you unless you have a go. I would encourage you to follow the prompting of your heart. If God gives you a vision or a dream, follow through with it and He can work through you in ways you can't even begin to imagine, even though you may not think that you are capable or equipped to do it.

TERRY

Finally 'Mr Right' did come along. Terry had grown up in the South Australian country town of Whyalla, where he had worked and studied as an electrical apprentice with the BHP. He excelled in his studies and won an Apprentice of the Year award and a trip to

Melbourne. His lifelong dream was to become an electrical engineer and he had his future all planned out to complete his studies at university in Adelaide. However, when he became a Christian he was involved in his local church in Whyalla and eventually felt that God called him to the ministry. He gave up his plans to attend university and instead enrolled in Crusade Bible College in Adelaide.

Terry and I met when he was studying in Bible College, and I was working in the church office. When he asked me out on our first date he said that he had some problems he wanted to talk over with me. We didn't get to discuss those problems on our date, but they later became evident as our relationship developed. Terry and I found that, besides a strong mutual attraction and getting on well together, we both had a deep desire to serve God. Terry had an enquiring mind and loved history and English literature. Although he'd been a bit of a rebel at High School his attitude had changed under the tutelage of a gifted Latin teacher who imparted to him a love of language and literature. I respected Terry's depth of knowledge of the Bible and of spiritual things, his desire to serve God and his understanding of world events and God's plan for the nations. Although Terry was troubled by various emotional problems I believed that God had all the answers and that nothing was too hard for Him to solve. Terry and I were married in 1969, when I was twenty nine, twelve months after we started dating.

We were very much in love, and excited about

the life ahead of us. Six months after we were married Terry resigned from a good job as an electrical sales representative, I resigned from my position at the church office, and we moved to Mildura in northern Victoria to assist in the pastoral ministry in a newly established church there. The only work Terry could obtain was in the haberdashery section of a Department store, which was rather a change from the tough environment of the steel works in BHP Whyalla. We had many a laugh as he grappled with mastering the intricacies of buttons and zips and even came to understand ladies bra sizes. I secured a job in a solicitor's office, and we put our hearts and souls into helping in the church. A momentous event for us was the purchase of our first house. We couldn't wait for our furniture to arrive, so we slept on the floor for the first few nights just to be in our own home.

Like many newlyweds, Terry and I discovered that we had quite different personalities. He was artistic and sensitive whereas I was pragmatic and down to earth. Consequently, although being in love, we had adjustments to make as we learnt to live together, as do most married couples. However, as well as these normal adjustments, Terry often found it difficult to handle my intrusion of his personal space. He would become extremely annoyed over some minor issue that had upset him, and react with anger and frustration because he could not cope with it. Sometimes he would become depressed, say that he needed space, and then 'shut down' and not speak to me for days. Then sometimes he would be extremely loving, affectionate and caring. As a new bride I found this see-sawing of emotions hurtful and hard to cope with, or to understand. Terry's explanation was, "This is just the way I am. You'll have to learn to live with it." It was how he had learned to cope and survive with emotional issues - to withdraw until he gained control within himself. This was not at all what I had expected of marriage.

We returned to Adelaide after eighteen months so that Terry could receive counselling and prayer from Leo Harris, in our home church, because he had become extremely depressed and, at times, almost suicidal. Terry found a new job teaching electrical apprentices at the Technical College in Adelaide, which brought him great satisfaction. He loved to teach and enjoyed the student contact as well as his involvement in assisting in the writing of a text book as part of the teaching curriculum. I returned to work in the church office.

Over several years Terry received intensive ministry and counselling. I believe that part of the cause of his emotional problems was due to a number of unresolved traumas he experienced during his formative years. I am sure that this would now be recognised as post traumatic stress disorder, and the pain of the suppressed emotions would explain his periodic outbursts of frustration and anger, and the extreme mood swings that he experienced throughout his adult life.

During this time, he began to lecture in Bible College, teaching subjects such as Bible History and

Prophecy, and Public Speaking, which were dear to his heart. Although he fought many personal, spiritual and emotional battles throughout his life, his heart was to serve God, to teach and encourage others in their Christian faith, and to help people overcome problems and find fulfilment in their lives.

CARROL

In 1975 a young woman came to our church in a desperate condition. She was on the verge of a complete mental and nervous breakdown, caused by an abusive childhood and marriage. She had a new-born baby, Naomi, and little Carrol, only eighteen months old, and could not cope with the pressures of life and the care of her children. One family took the mother in to try to nurse her back to health, the baby was adopted by a family who moved to New Zealand shortly afterwards, and toddler Carrol came to us. All Carrol had was a cardboard box with a few clothes in it, a bottle, an old well worn teddy and a plastic inflatable chair.

I realised that this dear little girl needed us and we wanted to care for her, but I had to be sure that this was the right decision for her and for us, and so I asked God for his guidance and wisdom. He clearly spoke to my heart through the verse in the Bible in Matthew 18:5, *"Whoever welcomes a little child like this in my name welcomes me"* (NIV). We welcomed Carrol into our home and she walked right into our hearts.

Carrol was a troubled and fearful little girl when

she first came to us because she had been through many traumatic experiences in her short life. However, through much prayer, and lots of loving, she gradually settled in to our home and brought us much joy. It was wonderful to see her blossom in her new-found security.

A few months later I took Carrol for a routine check-up with our local doctor and he was alarmed to discover that she had a serious heart murmur. On checking her medical records we found that this had been diagnosed at birth by a leading Adelaide heart specialist, but had not been treated or monitored since that time. When we took her to see the specialist he was extremely concerned and told us she would be in a wheelchair by the time she was a teenager if she did not have surgery to correct her heart condition.

We needed to get Carrol's mother's permission to have the surgery, and when we approached her the two questions she asked were: "Will she have a scar?" and, "Will she be able to wear a bikini?" We assured her that if she didn't have the surgery she would be in a wheelchair so she wouldn't be able to wear a bikini anyway. She gave her approval and we put Carrol through major heart surgery at two and a half years of age. She looked so tiny and helpless after the operation, lying in a huge oxygen tent, hooked up to monitors, with many tubes protruding from her little body, but she made a marvellous recovery and was home in just over two weeks, healthy and well again.

MINISTRY IN CANBERRA

Terry seemed to have resolved some of the major problems that had bothered him. We were still keen to serve God, and in light of this we embarked on a trip to the eastern states, visiting various churches along the way, asking God for his direction for our lives. Our hearts were touched by the church in Canberra. Terry felt that it was a strategic place because of his strong belief that God had a plan and purpose for the nation of Australia. We received an invitation to come and assist in pastoral ministry in the church in Canberra and, after much prayer and soul searching, in late 1976 we gave up our jobs once again, packed up all our belongings and set off to serve God in this new place.

We received a small allowance from the church, and signed up to rent a house, without a full-time job or the means to provide for our family. Fears that I had suffered as a child in regard to financial insecurity surfaced and took hold of my mind, and I became so fearful that I did not sleep for two weeks. There is a great difference between the everyday fears that we are all subject to and can overcome by a positive attitude and by trusting in God's promises, and that overpowering all-encompassing fear that consumes your thinking and cannot be reasoned away. I sought help from the senior pastor of the church who prayed with me, and I was wonderfully set free from this fear and never troubled by it again.

After trying unsuccessfully to earn a living by

selling encyclopedias, Terry was thrilled to secure a position at the local College of Technical and Further Education (TAFE) teaching electrical apprentices once again. He also assisted in pastoral and teaching ministry in the church, and I worked in the church office.

SHARON

The week after we moved to Canberra we were befriended by a young couple in the church and, in the course of conversation over a meal at their home, we shared with them that we had been hoping and trying to have a child for seven years. By this time I was thirty six. Our new friends said that they had great success in praying for couples to conceive and would pray for us. To our delight, a few months later we found out that I was pregnant, and in October 1977 our daughter Sharon was born. What joy she brought and continues to bring to our lives. I loved every minute of my pregnancy and the experience of giving birth, because I had just about given up hope that it would ever happen for us. The wonder of bringing a new life into the world is to me the most profound and enriching experience. Carrol was thrilled with her new baby sister and was proud to show her off to her friends. We hoped that we would now be able to have more children. However, this did not eventuate, and we came to accept that our family was complete with our two beautiful girls.

Imagine our surprise therefore in 1983, when I had been feeling ill for some weeks and thought that I had the flu, only to discover that I was pregnant again at forty three years of age. It took a few weeks for us to get used to the idea, and then we became really excited and began to make plans. However, I miscarried at three months. The miscarriage was more traumatic for me than the actual birth of a baby because there was a lot of pain and discomfort, but no thrill of the new life to follow. I came to understand the sadness of other mothers who suffer miscarriages. However, I felt the comforting presence of God during this time, as well as the loving support of family and friends.

We decided that I should work part-time to supplement our income and in 1979 I began to work on Friday mornings in the Classifieds section of the Canberra Times. I enjoyed the work and the company of the other women, and have continued to work there part-time for the past twenty seven years. The work has changed considerably over the years. When I started at the Canberra Times we worked in a confined area on electric typewriters, and the noise level of telephone conversations and typewriters clacking away made it difficult to hear the customers. This has now progressed to where most of our work is done through the fast, quiet and (usually) efficient electronic medium of computers.

I never cease to wonder at what one can do with a computer compared to my early office experiences. I started work in an office in 1955 when I was fifteen. We pounded away on the keys of manual typewriters and rubbed out, or dabbed lots of white-out on to the pages for corrections. If you got it wrong you had to start all over again. Oh, the speed with which we can now cut, copy and paste in one or two strokes of the keyboard. How awesome are the speedy communication we can have through emails and faxes. When my father was a bank manager all the ledgers and figures were hand written and added up in the head. Dad was faster than a calculator, but I don't think he could beat a computer. I am sure if he were alive today he, too, would marvel at the speed of Excel.

TRIUMPHS AND TRAUMAS

Terry and I were involved in pastoral care in a number of churches, and eventually in 1981 we were approached by a small group of people to start Bible studies in our home. We soon outgrew our home as more and more people started to come to the meetings. We formed a church known as Shekinah Christian Centre with Terry being the senior pastor. (It is now known as Ginninderra Christian Church.) It was a close-knit community of people with a special emphasis on fellowship, relationships and encouragement. God was gracious and blessed the church with enthusiastic and dedicated members and a gifted and committed ministry team. A number of people became Christians and grew in their relationship with God. One lady wrote recently:

> *"When we first came to Canberra in 1984 our daughter was invited to church by her young friend Carrol, the minister's daughter, where she was shown friendship and acceptance – as were the rest of the*

family when we also began to attend the church. I had never experienced such overwhelming warmth and absorption – I just felt surrounded by love on my first visit to the church. The love and grace of God was demonstrated to our family by the people in the church as they took the time to care, and ease the years of hurts and feelings of unworthiness. I was in a pit of despair before I was drawn into God's family. That tangible evidence of God's love, grace, mercy and forgiveness shown to me was literally life-giving and turned my life around."

In his personal life and in the home Terry was still at times subject to periods of depression and discouragement, sometimes resulting in unprovoked outbursts of frustration and anger. He would then be filled with guilt and remorse as he knew how hurtful this was to the family and that it was not right. Sometimes he would become suicidal and would then seek counselling and help from other senior pastors in our denomination. This seemed to be a cycle that was repeated over the years. I wondered at times if another contributing factor for this could have been his intense involvement as a teenager with the occult, in its many different forms, before he became a Christian If we dabble in occultish practices those spiritual powers can often obtain a foothold in our lives. Today people think that things such as tarot cards, séances, fortune tellers and witches are harmless fun and even introduce them to children's parties. They don't realise that they are dabbling with real spiritual powers that can have lasting effects on their lives.

On one occasion, Terry shut himself in the dark in his study for days until he came out of his depression. For some reason Christmas seemed to be a bad time for him, although I never discovered the reason why. It was often difficult for me to make Christmas the happy occasion it should have been for our children. I found it extremely hard to keep the peace in the home and to protect the girls from the fall-out. I tried to reach out to Terry at these times but found that I couldn't get past the defensive barriers he put up. After one especially bad day the entry in my journal reads, "Even though the tears on the outside have dried up I am still crying on the inside. I can feel the tears flooding my heart."

Depression is now being acknowledged as a common illness that needs to be treated. Recently a number of people holding prominent public positions have openly stated that they suffer with depression, and are taking time out to get the help needed for them to recover. The pressures of public life can greatly exacerbate these problems, since the person seeks to put on a public face while all the time battling the 'black dog' of depression, as it has been so aptly named. Sadly, many times families pay the price at home, as we did. Those who are the closest and dearest are the ones who bear the brunt of the frustration and anger, at great cost to the relationship. Perhaps this is because the sufferer feels that it is the only 'safe' environment where they can vent their pent-up feelings. Some people suffering with depression have taken their own lives in suicide because they were unable to cope.

On looking back over the twenty nine years of our marriage, and the cycles of depression Terry suffered, I wonder how different life would have been if it had been recognised and treated properly. He was a very gifted man, who could have achieved so much more if he had been able to break free from the shackles of his depression and emotional problems. He struggled at times to continue with his ministry in the church, which he dearly loved, when he helped other people to overcome their problems while battling these personal issues within him. Hopefully, with the greater public awareness, others will be able to recognise these symptoms and seek the help that is now available.

Despite these traumas we also had many good family times. We were closely involved with the girls in their activities. We bought Carrol a horse when she turned thirteen, as horses were her consuming passion in life right from when she was a little girl. We were involved in all the horse-related events, including gymkhanas, shows, and riding lessons. Even though Terry was not a horse lover he would get up early and help Carrol catch her horse and float it to various shows, where we would all cheer her on in her events.

Sharon was involved in Irish dancing, also from an early age, and we often attended local Irish Dancing competitions when she competed, as well as travelling interstate for major dancing events. These were fabulous occasions with many talented dancers from all over Australia wearing exquisitely embroidered dresses and dancing to beautiful Irish music. It was spectacular entertainment, which we enjoyed long before Riverdance became popular. Terry took many hours of videos of the girls in their elected activities and we were both immensely proud of their achievements.

One of the things that brought me great pleasure over the years was running Bible study groups for the women in the church, as well as being involved in Sunday School, the children's and youth ministry, and administrative work for the church. I formed many deep and lasting friendships while we shared our hearts and lives through the daily challenges that came to all of us. Another exciting opportunity became available to present the Christian message in our local school through a Bible Club which large numbers of children enthusiastically attended.

Church family camps were a great time of inspiration and relaxation. One of my tasks was to endeavour to get everyone involved in the Saturday night camp concerts, which usually turned out to be hilarious events and uncovered many hidden talents from previously shy and retiring church members. Terry and I had a lot of fun putting on silly skits together. It is wonderful how therapeutic an evening of hilarity and laughter can be. Barriers of reserve and formality crumble when people relax and have fun as they laugh together.

Getting alongside people and encouraging them to achieve their dreams and overcome their problems was particularly fulfilling for me. I was able to encourage others through a lesson I learnt when I was younger. I had become anxious and depressed over some difficult situations in my life, and the heavens seemed as brass. My prayers were not being answered and I began to doubt the existence of God. After some weeks of heart searching and prayer I had a revelation that has been undergirding my life since that time. The scripture that spoke to my heart was – *"man does not live on bread alone, but on every word that comes from the mouth of God"* Matthew 4:4 (NIV). Our feelings can change, our circumstances change, people change, but God's Word never changes, and if we trust in Him and in His Word He will always sustain us and eventually bring us through our difficulties.

TRIP OF A LIFETIME

In March 1985 Terry decided to give up his position at the TAFE so that he could devote more time to the church. However, before he took up the position of full-time ministry, we decided to take his two months long service leave, sell our car, and travel overseas. I was conscious that my father had saved and planned and dreamed of travelling in his retirement, but serious ill health had made that impossible and he had not long retired before he passed away after a debilitating fight with emphysema. I am so glad now that Terry and I seized the opportunity when we had it. We decided not to take Carrol and Sharon with us because we were spending most of the time travelling, including a bus tour around Europe, so some friends from the church moved into our home with their young family and looked after the girls while we were away.

It had long been a dream of ours to go to places we had read about in history books and in the Bible, and so we had the trip of a lifetime. We went to Egypt with all its wealth of ancient history, travelled up the Nile and walked around and down into the great pyramid. We spent ten days in Israel and steeped ourselves in its heritage of Biblical history as we sat by the sea of Galilee, walked through the narrow streets of the old city of Jerusalem, saw the place at Qumran where the Dead Sea Scrolls were found, visited Masada, swam in the Dead Sea – or should I say floated amongst various items of unpleasant flotsam, visited Bethlehem, Jacob's well, Nazareth and many other places we were so familiar with from the Bible stories we had read over the years.

The highlight of our time in Israel was when we participated in the dawn service on Easter Sunday morning at the Garden tomb in Jerusalem, along with three thousand other visitors from countries all over the world. This was followed by the great privilege of attending a church service to hear Richard Wurmbrand, the humble man who had been imprisoned in Romania for over twenty years for being a Christian pastor and had suffered unspeakable torture for his faith. I had read many of his books, including *Tortured for Christ*. He began his sermon with these words: "I apologise to you all for wearing slippers while preaching. I am sure that you must find this unusual, but because of all the beatings I endured on the soles of my feet I can no longer find any shoes that will fit my misshapen feet." These were just some of the many scars that he bore on his body with the pride that he had been counted worthy to suffer for his faith.

Our last evening in Jerusalem was spent enjoying a coffee at the Intercontinental Hotel on the Mount of Olives watching the sun set over the ancient city. This was provided by the generous gift of a friend who had spent time there previously and said it was a must.

During our time in Egypt and Israel I became ill and, despite taking medication, my condition worsened. Eventually the people at the hostel in Jerusalem where we were staying strongly recommended I see a doctor. Fortunately the doctor spoke English, so he was able to understand my description of the symptoms. He diagnosed gastroenteritis and severe dehydration and put me in hospital for twenty four hours on a drip to re-hydrate my body. This was a nerve-wracking experience because none of the nursing staff could speak English and they didn't seem to be interested in trying to understand my antics when I endeavoured to get them to bring me a drink. When I finally managed to get someone to understand my request, their response was, "Kitchen closed".

The next day I felt much better, for which I was extremely grateful since we then headed off for a fairly gruelling thirteen day bus tour of Europe. It was one of those lightning trips where, if you dozed off on the bus for an hour or so, when you woke up you discovered that you had missed Germany or some other country or sight. We spent two weeks in the United Kingdom, visiting places of family interest to both Terry and me, especially the orphanage in Birmingham where his father lived as a child before coming to Australia. Being an avid student of history, Terry was fascinated by the great buildings and historic sights we saw in places such as Rome, Florence, Venice and, of course, London.

****

We returned from our trip and put all our energies into growing the church, with the help of our committed and enthusiastic members. People came to faith in Christ, were set free from problems in their lives, and marriages were restored. I believe that because Terry experienced many problems in his own life he was able to reach out to others with compassion and understanding.

We were also involved with the forming of the National Freedom Council, which aimed to help victims of injustice, along with a number of other organisations that sought to have a Christian influence in the political scene. These organisations held regular prayer meetings to pray for our nation and for its leaders.

When Carrol entered her teenage years she began to seek her independence and challenge our authority and values, and this caused greater tensions in our home, particularly between Carrol and Terry. We were concerned for her safety and well-being, and tried to warn her of pitfalls ahead. At times Terry could be compassionate and understanding. At other times, while struggling with his own problems, he had little patience with adolescent behaviour and would be harsh and authoritarian. This caused many major conflicts and traumas. It seemed a bit like World War Three at times! I tried to keep the peace and meet the needs of my children and my husband. Many times the emotional tension was so great I felt it as a physical pain in my body.

BRUSH WITH CANCER

I had experienced various problems with my bowel over the years, which I am sure was partly due to stress, and in 1987 after exploratory surgery, the doctor called me in to his surgery and spoke those words that strike fear into the hearts of so many, "Mrs Hipkiss, we have found traces of malignancy in your test results and we think you should see a specialist." Although initially I was shocked, I was quietly confident that God would be with me and felt uplifted and strengthened as friends and family members supported me in prayer. I asked God to bring me through this crisis and let me live to see my two girls grow up. I knew that God could heal me, and I also knew that He worked through doctors to treat illness.

I saw a bowel specialist in Sydney who booked me in for major bowel surgery at the Seventh Day

Adventist Hospital to remove the whole of the rectum, which was covered with a carpet of polyps, and to create a temporary colostomy to allow the bowel to heal.

I wrote in my journal the night before the operation, "*I have felt all along that the Lord has been quietly directing procedures. The doctor has a good reputation, the hospital is a Christian place where prayer begins every shift and operation, and the staff are very caring. It has a peaceful atmosphere, and there are Christian books and Bibles throughout the hospital ... I know that God wants me to be well and if I have to have an operation then I know that the divine surgeon will be there alongside the human one and that his power will effect the complete healing.*" After the surgery I was delighted to hear the good news from my specialist that, although the tumour was much larger than expected, after extensive testing they could find no further traces of malignancy.

I returned home to recuperate after the operation and to learn how to care for the colostomy. This was difficult as my skin reacted badly to the bag, which had to be changed a number of times each day. Many times I would have to stick the bag back onto raw skin, which was extremely painful. I was glad to return to Sydney three months later to have the colostomy reversed, even though it meant another major operation, two weeks in hospital, and a recovery period learning how to manage a difficult bowel. When the specialist discharged me from the hospital he said, "When you go home I want you to live quietly and without stress, as your bowel is greatly affected by any trauma." Well, that was a bit difficult in the circumstances!

TURNING AWAY

Eventually, after being in the ministry for twenty years, Terry walked away from the church in absolute discouragement and consumed by feelings of total failure. He became angry with God and turned his back on his faith for the next ten years. I believe that one poignant experience had particularly distressed and discouraged him. A beautiful young woman, a wife and mother with two small daughters, after years of suffering with severe depression and travelling to India and other places seeking to find answers, had come to our church and had discovered a vibrant faith and a wonderful new life. When she developed a brain tumour and died within a short period of time, Terry felt that he had failed her, and that God had let him down. He lost sight of the fact that she had found an incredible peace and direction for her life that she had never known before, and had been searching for all her life. He felt personally responsible that he had not been able to pray for her and see her recover, and he couldn't seem to find the answer to this. He said that he didn't understand why and therefore couldn't believe or trust in God any more.

Many of the people in the church wrote letters to Terry expressing their appreciation for his ministry and the ways in which he had helped them. One person wrote, "*I want to thank you for the time that I have known you as my pastor and I'm glad that you were there through that very important time of my life when I became a Christian… I really enjoyed the First Principles classes I attended and your enthusiasm about what you were teaching us … the things I learnt opened up a whole new area of life for me … I know it is Jesus who has changed my life, but it was through Shekinah Christian Centre that I have this whole new life and I feel like a new person.*"

However Terry could not accept it. As he later wrote, "*I became more and more discouraged … and doubted my value and self worth … eventually I rejected God and the ministry itself. I turned my back on God and with this rejection came rebellion, and then my pride would not allow me to go back. I had to prove that I could succeed without Him and without anyone else.*"

One night Terry became extremely depressed and, after a violent outburst of anger directed towards me and the girls, I felt that the time had come for me to take a stand and say, "Enough is enough." When he had driven off in the car, which he often did at those times, I bundled the girls into my car and took them to a friend's home. I rang Terry and said that I felt we should separate until we could resolve these difficulties. I told him that although I loved him and knew that he was in pain himself, I could not accept his behaviour and the toll it was taking on our family any longer. It was as if I had drawn a line in the sand and said, "This has to stop." I had finally stood up on the inside, and by doing so regained my self-esteem and confidence.

The saying that came to my heart at the time was, "To thine own self be true". Terry moved out of the home and left me a letter saying that he was sorry, that he loved us and hoped and prayed that we could resolve these issues.

I believe that the principle of husband and wife living in loving submission to one another is important to a successful and happy relationship, but I also believe that we can still have a loving and submissive heart while refusing to yield to destructive anger and verbal abuse, no matter what the cause may be. Our separation lasted only for three months, but after we got back together Terry never again stepped over that line into abusive anger. He agreed to see a counsellor to try to resolve the problems within the home and marriage and attended a few counselling sessions, but he was not able to cope with the emotional pain of dealing with those past traumas and so didn't follow through with it any further.

I continued my involvement with the people in the church, all of whom were loving and supportive of our family. One of the regular events of our ladies' groups over the years was our clothing swap, held once every school term, when the women brought in clothing and goods that they no longer needed, spread them out over a large table, and then went through them and took home anything they wanted or could use. We were constantly surprised at how many bags of clothes and assorted goods were left over, which we would then take to one of the local charity bins.

Each time this happened I would say, "We have so much clothing we should start an Opportunity Shop!" Eventually the idea took hold and a group of us got together and, after much prayer and with encouragement from the pastor of the church, we said, "Let's do it!" We did all our sums, worked out how many pieces of clothing we would have to sell to pay the expenses, found a local shopping centre with a vacant shop to rent and in June 1990 Hand to Hand Opportunity Shop began, and still continues today. The shop is staffed by voluntary helpers and all the profits are given away to needy people, charitable organizations, and overseas missions. Over $400,000 has been given away to date. It is amazing what can be accomplished with a small group of committed and faithful people who are willing to give freely of their time and efforts to help others.

In that same year I was surprised and delighted when Terry told me that he had sent away for an application form for us to attend an Anglican Marriage Encounter weekend. He knew that this had been a desire of my heart for many years. On our weekend retreat we began to communicate in a way that we had never done before. The couples who led the weekend taught us how to share our feelings about situations in ways that were constructive rather than destructive.

This wonderful new depth of communication in our relationship continued for some months, and I brimmed with hope that we had taken major steps to overcome our problems. Then, as we began to talk about sensitive issues, Terry once again withdrew, shut down and said that he didn't want to continue with our dialogue. He said that it was too painful and intrusive. However he did want to maintain our involvement with the Marriage Encounter Community because he felt the warmth of their loving acceptance of him. This continued for a number of years and the people in the Marriage Encounter Community faithfully supported us in prayer.

After Carrol married and left home we decided to take in overseas home-stay students. Over the years since then students from Australia, Hong Kong, Taiwan, China, Japan, Korea and Fiji have lived in my home for varying periods from five weeks up to three years. These girls have fitted in beautifully with our family and have always been courteous and extremely conscientious students, working hard at their studies. It was a wonderful cross-cultural experience for Sharon during her teenage years when she learnt to communicate with and relate to young women of different cultures and languages.

As well as continuing with Irish dancing during her teenage years, Sharon also participated in performances with Sonseekers, a group of children and young people who presented the gospel message with great enthusiasm through song, dance and drama. Their experiences while travelling on tours through New South Wales and then to Fiji, were challenging and inspiring, both to the group and those they ministered to. She also had the great experience of being part of a team of young people who went on a mission trip to Indonesia.

For a number of years Terry went through an extremely stressful time in his work as a TAFE teacher. Without the extra pressures of church ministry he managed to cope, although it took its toll on his health, which he believed was a contributing factor to his later illness. He filled his spare time with various activities such as singing and performing with the TAFE players, joining a fossicking club and spending weekends away camping in the bush, along with other hobbies such as calligraphy and cooking. He loved nothing better than to invite our friends over for a meal and cook up a banquet of his latest culinary discoveries. We lived together more as companions than husband and wife over those ten years. One mutual interest we shared during this time was spending time with our children and grandchildren. Our grandchildren brought a new dimension of loving to our lives, and helped us to see the world again from a child's perspective, with their innocence, love and affection.

During this time God whispered into my heart some words of encouragement that I wrote in my journal and read over many times. One of these was:

"My child, I love my wayward and rebellious children just as I love my obedient and faithful children. As Moses was in the desert for forty years, so Terry will remain in separation from me and my love, but in the end he will feel the pull and tug of my love in his heart."

We all face many challenges in life. Some I faced over the years were: how to love unconditionally, without appearing to give approval to unacceptable behaviour; how to express love to someone who continually pushes you away; and how to build your child's self esteem when harsh negative words have been spoken over them. Just because we are Christians doesn't mean that we have a trouble free life of perfect peace and harmony. Challenges in all shapes and sizes come to most people, whether they are Christians or not. As has been said, bad things happen to good people. The difference is that we can turn to God in prayer during the difficult times and He will comfort and strengthen us, even if the answers don't come straight away. He promises to help us to have patience, grace and perseverance. We can find God's wisdom and His strength and, with the counsel and encouragement of friends and a sense of humour, we can come through these difficult times. Someone once said, "God is more interested in our character than our comfort."

I am thankful for the wonderful Christian friends who listened, supported and encouraged me, and prayed for our family. I am particularly thankful for the strong foundations undergirding my life through the loving nurture and care I received from my parents in my formative years, for this stood me in good stead through the difficult times. Without that inbuilt self esteem I am sure I would have not survived the years of negativity and criticism. It was a great blessing to me to know that my Mum faithfully prayed for me daily, as she did for each of her children.

I have found humour is a great tension reliever. Even in the midst of stressful situations we can often find something to laugh about. Terry had a quirky sense of humour. He was fond of puns, and although our ideas of humour were quite different, we still enjoyed many a good laugh together. A dear friend, who has since passed away, was a fun loving lady. In the midst of all the stresses in her life, including a long battle with cancer, she could always find some funny angle that would have us both in stitches of laughter. I urged her to write a book on some of her life's experiences and she said that if she did she would call it *"Gathering gold dust on the way to Glory."* Unfortunately she went to glory before she got to write her story.

The Bible says that laughter is like good medicine for us. That's why I love Barbara Johnson's books. She faced such incredible pain and sadness, especially in relation to her four sons, with the loss of one son through the Vietnam War, another through a drunk driver, and another who was separated from her for many years. In the midst of all the traumas of her life she could always find something to laugh about. She literally built joy into her life. Somehow, in the midst of pain, to read her books brings light and laughter to an otherwise dark and gloomy situation. As my friends and I have grown older we have shared great hilarity over some of our senior moments. A sense of humour certainly brightens our days and keeps things in perspective.

FINDING THE WAY BACK

After ten years of being away from the church and his faith in God, Terry became seriously ill with prostate cancer, which eventually developed into bone cancer. He knew that he was dying and told me that he wanted to come back into a relationship with God, but couldn't seem to find the way and didn't want people to think he was clutching at straws because he was facing death.

Terry decided he wanted to visit Adelaide for the last time to say farewell to his family. While we were there he experienced attacks of excruciating pain and was admitted to hospital to try to get some relief. During the night in his hospital room he woke up suddenly and heard someone say, "I don't understand, but I believe." He looked around the hospital room to see who had spoken. There was no-one else there. Then he realised he had spoken out of his heart while waking from sleep. In his heart he then heard God say to him, "Welcome home, son." The open arms of God enfolded Terry with His love. Although he didn't have all the answers, Terry was now content to trust in God and rest in his faith.

His renewed love for God transformed Terry's life and we had a precious six months together as a family when emotional wounds were healed and relationships restored. He asked my forgiveness for the things that had happened over the years that he knew were not right. He apologised to the girls for the hurts they had suffered. Through the grace of God forgiveness brought great healing. As Terry wrote, "*On looking back over my life, there are many things which I now deeply regret, and I am so thankful that I have had the opportunity to put matters right with my family and with God. Words cannot describe the grace of God and the peace that He gives us."*

His positive faith in God sustained him through his illness, even when he became paralysed from the waist down from the tumours pressing on his spine. He spent three months in the Hospice, where the loving care of the staff made it what I called, 'A little bit of heaven on earth'. He shared his faith with literally hundreds of people, in fact everyone who came to his bedside. He had no fear of death.

Terry had a great desire to worship God within a church service once again. This was difficult to arrange because of his paralysis and he needed a wheelchair and other special assistance. However, we finally managed to organise it. I sat beside him in the first church service he had attended for ten years and the tears rolled down his face as he sang the songs and worshipped God with all his heart. He died six days later and went home to be with the Lord. It was June 1998. Many hundreds of people came to his funeral to pay their respects and there they heard about the message of faith and hope that Terry had embraced once again.

****

At the time of Terry's death I didn't shed many tears. There seemed to be so many things to do that I was carried through in a kind of adrenalin rush. About a year later Sharon went through a sad and painful experience and in identifying with her pain it seemed like the floodgates of my heart were opened and all the grief within me poured out. I can remember crying so much while driving to work that I could hardly see the road. I think that I was grieving for the things that could have been and should have been. But I knew that in weeping there was healing and so I went with the flow and allowed God to heal the things in my life that needed His touch.

MINISTRY TO WOMEN

Over the years I have had the privilege of being involved in various areas of ministry to women. In recent times, over a period of about four years, I ran a support group for mothers who were having problems with their teenage and adult children. I was able to draw upon many of the experiences and lessons that I had learned over the years to encourage and support other Mums. I could confidently say to them, there is hope, there is strength, and there is wisdom, in God. One mother wrote to me:

"Coming to your house is like entering a haven for the hurting. A warm hearth on bitter days. We step over the threshold to a feeling of friendship, comfort and anonymity, and find somewhere to pour out our souls without judgement."

We saw many answers to prayer as these mothers shared their experiences in the group and gained support, wisdom and encouragement from each other.

A special time in my life was my involvement with the women's ministry in Grace Christian Fellowship, the church I was attending at the time. I found particular fulfilment in assisting the leader of the women's ministry in the areas of administration and planning. It was good to be part of a Committee where women with various gifting and abilities were given free expression under anointed leadership.

Around the same time I attended an Emmaus Walk, and found great inspiration and encouragement in hearing the stories of other women who had walked through stressful times in their lives, and had learnt much through their experiences, which they were able to share with others. I have since become closely involved with the Emmaus Community, which is comprised of people from many different churches and walks of life, and is a loving and caring group of people, with a heart to serve others.

*****

Carrol and her husband Joe and their five children live not far away from me, and I am thankful that I can have regular contact with them and spend time with my delightful grandchildren. Carrol remains just as passionate about horses – and all animals in general. Although busy with the full-time care of her family, she still finds time to look after her three horses that are on agistment on a farm nearby, along with cats and dogs and chooks and various other animals that seem to find their way to her place.

Sharon completed a Bachelor of Commerce at Canberra University and is currently working at the Department of Finance and Administration and completing her Master's degree. She and her husband Peter took leave from their jobs in 2004-2005 and spent a year working and travelling overseas. I was privileged to be able to travel to Taiwan to visit them in 2005 while they were living there. On my way home Sharon and I stayed for three days in Hong Kong and spent time with three of our original home-stay students, who are now all successful business women. Sharon and Peter have returned to work in Canberra and are now busily engaged in building their new home.

REFLECTIONS

I believe that every day we have on this earth is a gift from God that we should treasure and enjoy. This was especially brought home to me after my brush with cancer. None of us know when our time is up and our appointed day is come, so we should live each day as if it is our last and not put off doing those important things. We should seek to live in a close relationship with God and experience the peace of heart and mind that only He can give; spend quality time with friends and family; tell someone that we love them; write that letter expressing our thanks and appreciation; and forgive those who have hurt us.

My journey continues, along with the challenges and joys. The ongoing problems associated with the bowel surgery and managing a difficult bowel, adjusting to living on my own as a single person, releasing and letting go of adult children to live their lives independently, the delights of grandchildren and the special love they draw from us, getting my head around all the financial decisions that need to be made when facing retirement - all of these bring new challenges and I thank God He is with me every step of the way.

Each new experience we walk through is a learning experience: how to cope; what to do and what not to do; when to speak and when to keep silent. The wisdom we gain from our experiences is like a precious treasure that we can share with others along life's journey.

Throughout the years I have constantly been encouraged with words from the scriptures such as II Corinthians 12:9 where God says that His grace is sufficient for us in any situation; in Hebrews 13:5-6 we read that we need not be afraid for He will never leave us; and in Hebrews 4:16 He tells us to come boldly to the throne of grace to find help in a time of need.

As we draw on His sustaining grace in our daily lives to cope with the many different pressures that come upon all of us, so we are then able to share with others. Nothing, no experience, is wasted in God's economy. It says in Romans 8:28, "*And we know that in all things God works for the good of those who love Him,* who have been called according to His purpose" (NIV). So whatever you are walking through at the moment or have been through in the past, God is with you, He will never leave you, and He will use you to bless, encourage and strengthen others in similar situations. To conclude, the following are a few of the simple things that bring me great pleasure. Big and important events are wonderful, but the simple things of daily living are without price.

The warm and loving companionship of good friends

The feel of a child's hand trustingly holding mine

The sound of those words – "I love you Mum"

The beauty of a rose freshly picked from my garden

The smell of the ocean and the tingling feel of the cold salt water on my skin

Curling up in a warm bed on a cold night with a good book

The heart-warming welcome home from my little dog Tara

Hilarious laughter shared with friends over humorous moments

Smooth clean sheets on a freshly made bed

Warm feet in my cosy Ugg boots on a cold day

The security of driving a reliable and comfortable car

The easy flow of writing with a smooth flowing pen

Enjoying a cup of tea on a crisp sunny morning in my garden.

… these are just a few of my favourite things.

Robyn and Terry on their wedding day with Leo Harris, August 1969.

Robyn: before the wedding with her siblings and parents.

Cadet Crusaders – Robyn on the far right.

Robyn and
Terry with
Carrol and
Sharon.

(left) Robyn and Terry
in Egypt, March 1985.

Robyn with Sharon and Peter on their wedding day, with Carrol and Joe and their children, Jamie, Danielle, Tiffany and Stephanie, October 2002.

Robyn and Sharon at a reunion in Hong Kong with some of the earlier home-stay students. From left to right, Vivienne, Cammy and Alice, March 2005.